THE
SECRETS
—of—
NATURAL
NEW ZEALAND

VIKING

THE SECRETS of NATURAL NEW ZEALAND

Illustrations by Betty Brownlie
Text by Ronald Lockley

VIKING

VIKING

Penguin Books (N.Z.) Ltd, 182-190 Wairau Road, Auckland 10, New Zealand
Penguin Books Ltd, 27 Wrights Lane, London W8 5TZ (Publishing & Editorial)
and Harmondsworth, Middlesex, England (Distribution & Warehouse)
Viking Penguin Inc., 40 West 23rd Street, New York, New York 10010, U.S.A.
Penguin Books Australia Ltd, Ringwood, Victoria, Australia
Penguin Books Canada Ltd, 2801 John Street, Markham, Ontario, Canada L3R 1B4

First published 1987

Copyright © 1987 illustrations Betty Brownlie
Copyright © 1987 text Ronald Lockley

All rights reserved

ISBN 0 670 81248 X

A Shoal Bay Press book
Printed in Hong Kong through
Bookprint Consultants Ltd, Wellington

Contents

Preface

The purpose of this book is to illustrate both the natural history and the natural beauty of the New Zealand countryside, with its scenic and pastoral attractions, in chapters depicting the rich variety of its flora and fauna in a dozen different habitats. As author of the text, I feel privileged to collaborate with the artist in this first extensive book of her exquisitely accurate and beautiful paintings and sketches.

If this book has a message for the reader, it is to illustrate and describe a countryside we have learned to love while exploring it from Cape Reinga in the north to Stewart Island and the sub-Antarctic isles of the far south. We hope to show thereby that the riches of New Zealand lie not in her sprawling cities, in which more than half her population is concentrated today, but that in a world largely over-populated and ill-fed, it is our fortune to be a small nation with abundant natural resources and spacious wilderness areas for outdoor recreation - sport, tramping, climbing, bird, plant and marine studies, geologising - available in the wide choice of mountain, forest, lake, river and sea coast locations depicted here.

New Zealand has many nature reserves and national parks, as well as State forest parks, in total covering more than 10 per cent of our land surface. Fortunately too, there are still some remote islands and islets offshore, strictly protected as reserves, where exotic, predatory mammals have never existed (or have been eliminated). Here natural succession, regeneration and interaction of the pristine flora and fauna (birds, bats, reptiles and flightless insects) may be viewed by the fortunate visitor as a living museum of the ecosystem or habitat before the arrival of the Maori with his dog and little Polynesian rat.

It was the botanist Leonard Cockayne, in his classic *New Zealand Plants and their Story*, published over seventy-five years ago, who truly remarked, 'no primitive [endemic] plant association is desecrated by a single foreign invader', an observation lately confirmed by studies in which we have taken part, notably on Little Barrier Island. (*See page 159*). When man and his four-footed camp followers are banished from the land and there are endemic trees to provide seed, that land reverts to original forest. The well-lit understorey, which is such an attractive feature of unravished forest with its soft covering of shrubs, ferns, orchids and mosses, reappears to the exclusion of alien species which invaded the soil during the late activities of man and his animals.

Nature abhors a vacuum. The wandering amateur naturalist is somewhat comforted to find that where the weak-winged and flightless birds and other endemic creatures (including giant native snails and insects) evolved in a mammal-less land, have vanished, or become rare, several introduced species have partly or wholly filled the ecological gap. These are better equipped to survive, having done so in coexistence with their natural enemies at home: cats, mustelids, rats and predatory birds. Particularly agreeable to the eye or ear, and a feature of open farmland today, are the charms of European goldfinches, greenfinches, redpolls and yellowhammers; the murmurations of starlings, so beneficial in devouring grass grubs; and larks singing abundantly in the sky. Another visitor around homesteads is the chaffinch, one of the few species which has adapted to living and nesting in gloomy plantations of radiata pine, described as 'ecological deserts'. These and several other introduced species have fitted successfully into the new food and territory niches available as a result of clearing land for farming and commercial forestry. Here the artist has depicted them in their self-selected environments.

Further welcome additions to our fauna and flora list are the self-introduced species, accepted thereby as indigenous rather than endemic. Almost all of these have arrived from or via Australia, crossing the Tasman Sea on the favourable prevailing wind (birds, an Australian bat, butterflies and other insects, airborne spores and seeds), rafted on floating logs (skinks and insects) or some, in the last 200 years, adventitiously aboard ships. This natural immigration of 'new' species to enrich our island fauna and flora is a continuing process as old as the land itself. Our mainland forests would in fact seem almost birdless but for the presence of certain Australian species, more nimble on the wing to escape pigs, rats, cats, ferrets, stoats and weasels than any of the anciently evolved and often flightless endemics. Such Australian species as the harrier or bush hawk, pied stilt, grey duck, fantail (a flycatcher) and grey warbler have thrived in New Zealand for at least a thousand years. But new immigrants still come from across the Tasman Sea. According to the Maori and the early Pakeha settlers, the silver-eye or wax-eye, *Zosterops lateralis*, was first seen about 1856, but it is now numerous in gardens, orchards, and all settled habitat with bush cover. In the present century several insects and butterflies have settled here; not all have been beneficial to the economy. Attractive birds such as the welcome swallow and the white-faced heron are dynamic Australian species which have colonised the length and breadth of New Zealand since the first individuals were recorded here about 1940. In the last thirty years two handsome Australian wading birds have arrived and are breeding freely - the spur-winged plover and the black-fronted dotterel.

With hindsight we are amazed at the facile manner in which white settlers in the last century introduced European, and some Australian, plants and animals almost indiscriminately in their attempt to establish the good life of the pastoral and stock raising conditions which supported their former European way of life. In 1835 Charles Darwin, pondering his theory of the survival of the fittest during his only visit to New Zealand, at the Bay of Islands mission station, forecast that the success of the more dominant immigrants, both imported and self-introduced (he particularly noticed rats) would result in the destruction of the delicate balance of 'the endemic productions which had reached a standard of perfection attained in long isolation'.

Conservationists regret the fact that New Zealand has lost more living endemic species than any other nation in the world, but we are obliged to live with the result. The weaker species have gone because they were too delicate. Today we strive to strike a balance by encouraging the rarer endemics in their remaining habitats, moving them if necessary to safer ones set aside as permanent reserves. And latterly, with more successful survival rates for certain birds, snails, insects, reptiles, and rare plants, nature in New Zealand has a fair prospect of preserving the present amalgamation of old and new flora and fauna - which is all our children will know.

To this end we wish to dedicate this book to the Royal Forest and Bird Protection Society, now become the largest and most influential voluntary association co-operating with the Wildlife Service in the environmental field and in promoting nature reserves and legislation to conserve wildlife. We urge every reader to support the society.

Ronald M. Lockley

The Midsummer Garden

A garden is a lovesome thing, God wot.
Thomas Edward Brown (1830-97)

T hus wrote T.E. Brown more than a century ago, expressing that spiritual peace and joy that we feel in a garden where the fruits of human endeavour and love for its living plants, useful or ornamental, provide unending interest. Brown was a priest, happiest to worship out of doors. In the same poem, *My Garden,* he protests:

> Not God in gardens! When the eve is cool?
> Nay, but I have a sign;
> 'Tis very sure God walks in mine . . .

We who love to study the natural scene admire and strive to understand the complexity of innumerable plants and animals living and interacting together - the ecology of a garden - especially in high summer. We are diverted less by the need to mow a lawn or hoe down weeds than by the visual flutterings and activities of birds and butterflies. We watch the bumblebee 'stealing' nectar from the huge and beautiful hibiscus bloom. This flower is designed to be pollinated by a bird or large butterfly brushing against its tall stigma, but the bee, seeking the nectar at the base, alights on the wide-open petals and unintentionally avoids this service which it pays to a smaller flower in return for nectar and pollen.

We are fascinated by the praying mantis sat upon a leaf which it matches in colour, alert to seize the unwary fly or leaf-hopper coming within snatching distance of the lightning, jack-knife strike of its saw-toothed forelegs. No wonder some observers write it down as *preying* mantis, although it was first named because of its 'hands' held folded as if in devout prayer.

Such comings and goings all the sunlit day! The garden air is full of the voices and wings of wild creatures, the humming, buzzing and stridulation of insects, the calls of nesting birds. Some wild birds sing throughout the summer, if their mate is still incubating - perhaps a second or third clutch - and when building the nest. Cock birds in general - sparrow and starling are exceptions - rarely help in nest-building, and so have more time to sing. They sing, we believe, as much out of *joie de vivre* (bursting good health and readiness to mate) as to advertise their presence on guard in the chosen nesting and feeding territory, ready to warn off and, if necessary, to drive away intruders.

Possession is said to be nine-tenths of the law in Man; in birds it gives courage and strength to attack the would-be invader of the home ground. We have seen a tiny warbler strike at a cat, and a wild duck drive an intruding harrier twice her size down into the water of her nesting territory while preventing the hawk from seizing her new-hatched ducklings.

You may be sure the mated hen on her nest listens to every call and song of her male. She must also hear the voices of rival males, but it is up to her mate to drive them away, as he surely will if he is a strong, experienced adult. Although birds have no morals in the human sense, the family bond is strong in some species and strongest in those where the sexes are most alike externally - as in many finches, warblers, and most seabirds. They share domestic duties; some cocks help to incubate and both sexes feed the young, so it is a disaster if one of the pair is predated. In our studies of local sparrows we had leg-banded in a suburb of Auckland, when one mated cock went missing, the widowed hen spent two days incubating alone, but she was uneasy and at intervals called from the entrance to her nest, then accepted the attentions of an unbanded cock, young by his less vivid black bib markings.

In species so faithful, the female or male is unable to raise a brood single-handed. By contrast, where the cocks have brilliant plumage and hens wear drab feathers (pheasants and game birds, certain waders, bower birds and birds of paradise are examples) the male is polygamous. He takes no further interest in the female after she has been mated, and she must rear the family entirely on her own.

Mated goldfinches

Observe the social behaviour of these charms of finches in your garden. Perhaps a group of adults and newly-fledged young alight to drink at a bird bath or lily pond. Goldfinches and redpolls weigh so little they often alight on a lily-pad to drink or splash-bathe. Like other finches, they feed most of the year on wild seeds, crushing these in their powerful bills to produce a nourishing pulp which, lubricated with saliva from intestinal glands, is fed to the brooding hen and nestlings. But as the nestlings grow, the parents seem instinctively to recognise they need protein. Both adults will collect small insects, ants and aphids to feed their young while they are in the nest (two weeks) and perhaps for another week of their first flight when they follow their parents and beg for food.

Young sparrows

The loud trilling 'swee-reeing' of the cock greenfinch is redolent of the summer garden and home orchard as he circles the warm air above with a deliberate, slow, seemingly unco-ordinated beating of his green and golden wings, advertising his joy and readiness to mate where he finds plenty of food in weedy ground and waste corners. Here, in the nearest tall hedge or bush, the hen builds a sometimes slovenly nest of any handy material, usually lining it with rootlets and animal hair. We found one greenfinch nest made externally almost entirely of green-plucked groundsel, the seeds of which are a favourite food. With their powerful, heavy bills greenfinches easily pluck and crush such hard seeds as sunflower and maize, with the tongue rejecting the husk so that it is blown away on the wind.

Already by midsummer the first families of garden birds are losing their drab brownish nest plumage and looking more colourful, more like adults. This is a time of plenty of food, and of learning how to find it. There is much leisure to socialise and, like human teenagers, they behave towards each other in a playful but exploratory manner. There is a distinct hierarchy or pecking order, the older juveniles on top. Families tend to fly about together, individuals recognised by their distinctive voices. Each has to learn its place in the flock and maintain 'individual safety distance' to avoid surprise attack from a more aggressive neighbour. The younger birds learn swiftly from and copy the behaviour of the adults who are watchful and experienced in survival. The response to the alarm call of an adult which sees an approaching predator is for the whole flock to take to the air. The danger over, the flock, led by the adults, settles again to cluster once more on a food source.

Tired with the long, hot day of feeding and social activities, all birds except the owl retire, some before dusk, to sleep profoundly during the brief hours of the midsummer night. Garden shrubberies are favourite roosting sites for small birds, especially the warmth and thick cover of tall bamboo thickets, conifer, acmena and tecoma hedges. Hens with eggs or young brood these against the bare skin of the lower breast and belly, an area which becomes naturally defeathered just before her eggs are laid. This brood spot remains naked until her progeny acquire enough feathers to keep themselves warm, at least during the day. By night, upon her nest the devoted mother shuffles her eggs or children warmly under the cloak of her feathers and wings, closing these tightly as her head sinks to a resting position for ease in sleep. This reduces the escape of body heat and also of body scent which might guide a prowling rat or other predator to smell out the nest.

On warm summer days well-grown nestlings do not need brooding. Both parents are now fully occupied in finding enough food to satisfy the growing appetites of their soon-to-be fledged brood. Each adult at this time may make several visits within the hour, thrust food into gaping maws, and afterwards fly away with the whitish capsules of jelly-like faeces, which it is careful to drop at some distance from the nest. This instinctive hygiene, and the neat faecal capsule, convenient for carrying in one piece, has considerable survival value in keeping the nest clean and inconspicuous to predators.

Young birds born in nests in the open and in well-lit cover at first make no or few sounds when they gape their mouths hungrily on the arrival of a parent with food, whose approach is just as silent, and by devious routes to deceive an enemy. In heavy rain one parent will screen young nestlings by brooding them, or, if they are grown large, may open wide the umbrella of its extended wings to keep them dry. Photographers who unkindly remove shielding vegetation which obstructs their view of the nest and thus expose the contents to the hot sun, have reported that after settling in their observation hide within camera range of the nest, they have been amazed to watch one parent return and alleviate the heat distress of the helpless young chicks. If these gasp with open mouths and throats palpitating to circulate air (birds are unable to perspire) the parent will stand above the nest with extended wings to throw a shadow upon them. Soon the adult may become distressed and gasping, until relieved by its partner. Intelligent, or just instinctive reaction to a given situation? The result is the same - beneficial for survival.

Starlings, kingfishers and other hole-nesting birds behave differently. Safe in their shady tunnels or dark recessses, the growing nestlings early become noisy as soon as they hear a parent arriving with food. The squawking cries we hear at dawn under the house eaves or in the nest-box we have hung in a tree indicate plainly that mother or father starling has arrived with a beak-load of wriggling worms, grubs or insects. The hungry nestlings guide their breakfast in the right direction with ecstatic vocal anticipation from the dark nursery. The parent is further guided in the dim light by the vivid colour of the opened gape. In the young starling this is bright canary yellow, with the flanges pale lemon. All birds born in dark situations start life with bright coloured white, crimson or yellow gapes.

The early rising birds catch the worms and other small life crawling in the dew before most of us are awake and abroad in the summer. Most carnivorous birds vary their diet with the fleshy fruits of wild and cultivated plants in season. Some of us admire birds sufficiently to allow them a share of ripe strawberries, raspberries and currants, arguing that they deserve these as wages for their control of noxious insects, snails and slugs which abound in every garden in summer.

Starling, thrush, blackbird, dunnock, magpie, even the lark from the nearby meadow are dawn visitors who run, walk or hop about the lawn, devouring myriads of nocturnally active insects and worms before these retreat below ground or under leaf cover. At this season thousands of winged insects, after months, even years, as larvae feeding on plant roots below the surface, hatch from their pupal cases to enjoy their brief day as perfect insects mating aerially under the sun. Hungry birds seem at times to be snatching up sweet nothings, so minute are some of the smaller flies, moths and beetles emerging in the first light of dawn.

Often the principal reason for this early emergence is because they are so small. If they were immediately exposed to the full heat of the midday sun their soft, untried wings and tender bodies would be shrivelled up. A typical example is the fruit-fly, *Drosophila*, inhabitant of decaying, fermenting vegetation and the compost heap, which breeds so rapidly that the whole life cycle occupies only two or three weeks. To take advantage of the dew the fruit fly needs to emerge a little before dawn, the hour of greatest humidity, in which its minute body surface can absorb sufficient moisture to resist the drying heat of the coming day.

Watch the thrush pause at intervals as it patrols the green sward. It turns its head sideways as if listening with one ear for movements under the ground. Can it hear the burrowing noise of worm or slug, or the struggles of newly-mature insects

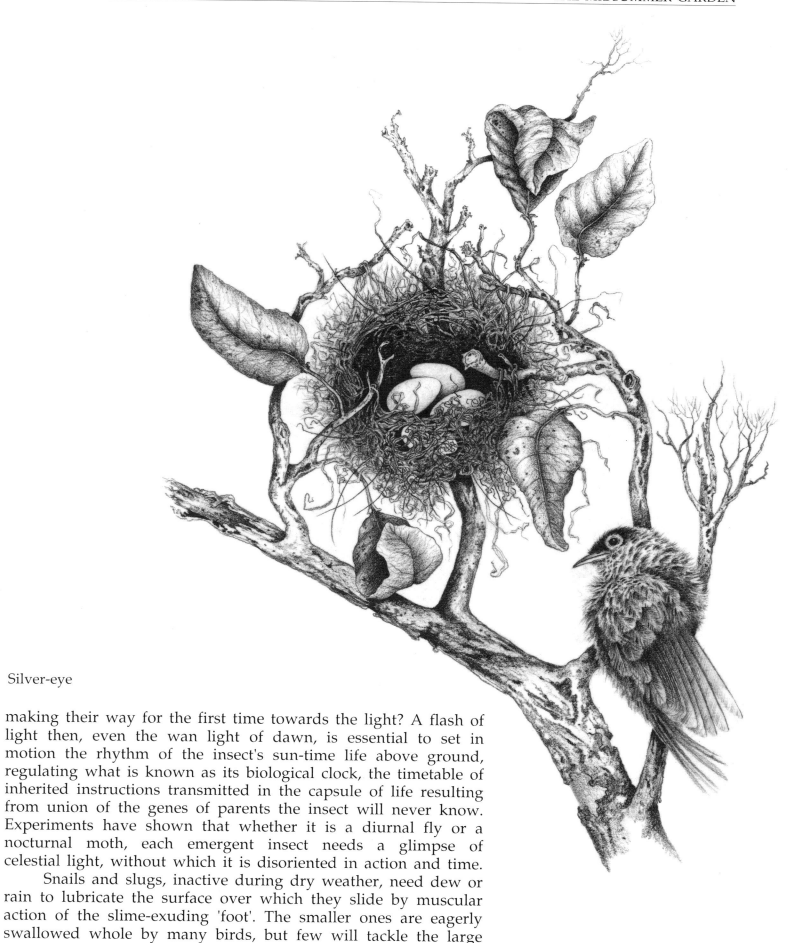

Silver-eye

making their way for the first time towards the light? A flash of light then, even the wan light of dawn, is essential to set in motion the rhythm of the insect's sun-time life above ground, regulating what is known as its biological clock, the timetable of inherited instructions transmitted in the capsule of life resulting from union of the genes of parents the insect will never know. Experiments have shown that whether it is a diurnal fly or a nocturnal moth, each emergent insect needs a glimpse of celestial light, without which it is disoriented in action and time.

Snails and slugs, inactive during dry weather, need dew or rain to lubricate the surface over which they slide by muscular action of the slime-exuding 'foot'. The smaller ones are eagerly swallowed whole by many birds, but few will tackle the large black or brown slugs which one meets on garden paths and lawn after rain or heavy dew. They seem repugnant to most of us, perhaps because of the viscid slime and faecal matter they trail. The large black slug is a scavenger of the bodies of other slug and insect casualties it may encounter.

The thrush is one of the few birds which knows how to extract a large snail from its shell. Using a stone or hard surface as an anvil, it pounds the shell against this until it is shattered. But often the cunning blackbird, which has not learned this art, watching perhaps from the cover of a bush, will dart forward and seize the snail body at the moment when the thrush is occupied in wiping snail slime from its bill. However, one experienced thrush in our garden has learned to avoid this black piracy by flying off with the snail to a more secret anvil within its feeding territory.

Fledgling thrush

Fallen nest (thrush)

Around the garden when birdsong almost ceases - the singers are busy raising their last broods before their postnuptial moult - the summer orchestra is more of an instrumental arrangement. Loudest of the players who love the hot sun are the cicadas. Thousands have emerged from their underground pupal cases. An almost deafening tintinnabulum is produced by the males, who bang their tambourine-like cymbals and hum an accompaniment by vibrating their transparent wings. The cymbals, technically known as 'tymbals', are a pair of flexible, horny plates hinged above a hollow chamber which acts as a resonator just below the waist. Muscles attached to the tymbals produce a variety of tunes and signals, according to the species, by buckling one tymbal at a time, separately, repeatedly, alternately, or both in unison. Cicadas listen with ears situated on their legs.

Over 4000 years ago the cynical Greek poet Xenarchus wrote: 'Happy the cicada lives, for he has silent wives!' However, the lovesick female (you may tell her from the male by the long ovipositor protruding from her abdomen) does sing sotto voce, a whispering 'come hither' which differs from each species but has the same intention. It immediately attracts the loud-singing male to fly alongside her and effect a silent nuptial embrace. The newly-mated female feeds greedily on plant juice, to nourish her developing eggs. She plunges her hollow stiletto - a kind of sucking straw - through the skin of plants, or the bark of shrubs. Her stomach visibly swells, and if the sap is that of a scented plant, such as a frangipani, an ambrosial aroma is wafted from the drops of sweet fluid oozing from the wound.

Ants, busy with their herds of aphid cows pastured on nearby plants, have a keen sense of smell, and may soon locate the cicada happily engrossed in her draught of sap. We have watched ants driving away small flies and other winged insects attracted for the same reason, which were busily lapping up the oozing drops around the cicada's stiletto. The greedy ants demand all. They tug at the cicada's beak, they bite her legs, and at last climb upon her back and attack her tender wings. They would soon cut her into 'takeaways', but Nature has provided

Thrush eggs (above) and blackbird eggs

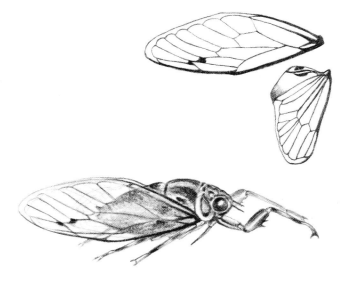

Cicada wing detail; adult cicada with sharp, strong, sap-sucking mouthpiece; cicada nymph.

Most species of garden ants tend herds of plant-sucking aphids for the sake of the sweet excretions of honeydew they exude, which ants feed on. There are well over fifty species of aphids troubling the gardener in New Zealand, and all have much the same extra-ordinary life cycle. Aphids overwinter on the host plant as eggs. From these hatch wingless females which throughout the summer reproduce several generations of virgin females by live birth (parthenogenesis). Huge populations build up, assisted by the curious fact that unborn progeny already have developing female embryos within them - that is, the virgin mother carries both virgin daughters and virgin grand-daughters in her reproductive system. The autumn generations are of winged virgins which take to the air and find a new host plant. Here they reproduce both winged males and females which mate and deposit fertile eggs. The male dies afterwards; he never eats, having no mouth parts.

Occasionally ants will eat an aphid, but most of the time they protect their honeydew 'cattle' by attacking the aphid's predators, spitting formic acid at those they cannot kill. This is no defence against the depredations of armour-clad ladybird beetles, the adults and young of which feed largely on aphids and related scale insects. The tough carapaces of ladybirds are handsomely spotted in various colours which are really a warning to would-be predators. If attacked by another insect, the ladybird will exude from its leg-joints an evil smell-ing yellow secretion with a bitter taste. Its appetite for aphids, scale insects, whitefly and red mite pests of garden and orchard is voracious enough to secure the ladybird an honoured place in biological warfare. When citrus crops in California and South Africa were attacked by a plague of scale insects, importation of the cardinal ladybird *Rodolia cardinalis*, from Australia and New Zealand, almost wiped out the problem in one year.

Ant society evolved several million years before thinking man appeared on earth. It is tempting to quote from Proverbs, vi,6: 'Go to the ant, thou sluggard; consider her ways and be wise', but we ought not to attribute human virtues or vices to animals. Considering the ant's perfection of organisation, where every ant is a slave under one giant mother ant, the wisdom they have achieved in all that time is disappointing, boring and bureaucratic. In the words of American writer Clarence Day, 'Ants are good citizens; they place group interest first, but carry it so far, they have few or no political rights, no vote - just duties.'

20

that a healthy pregnant cicada must first propagate her species before she dies - inevitable fate after she has laid her eggs, when she is no longer strong enough to resist such predation. She is equipped with an unusual deterrent device. As she rises in the air, shaking off her tormentors, she relieves herself of a copious discharge of urine, spraying it upon the assembled ants. This is a well-known defence mechanism when you disturb a well-fed cicada; it also lightens the burden of her bloated abdomen to make flight easier. The discomfitted ants run hither and thither, but will return to clean up the last drops of sap.

'Foolish one!' answers the ant of *Aesop's Fables* when the cicada comes to claim payment for her summer songs at the door of the ant's winter store, desiring food and shelter. 'You can fiddle a different tune now!' In our book of the *Fables* the ant is pictured, wearing a housewife's apron, blocking the entry of the supplicant who is attired in a big sunhat, violin under one arm, the other extended for her wages. We cannot easily dismiss that picture, engraved upon our youthful imagination, when we hear the last summer music of cicada and grasshopper, although we know that the next generation of noisy summer symphonists is already safely underground, newly hatched from her eggs. Cicada-grub beaks will be plunged (like those of the aphid cattle which the industrious ants will carry to pasture and stables below) into plant roots, to suck the rich sap all winter long.

The Old Woodshed

There are fairies at the bottom of our garden.
Rose Fyleman (1877-1957)

At the bottom of the farm garden a large old woodshed has long lost its door. Trees and climbing plants drop their leaves and twigs softly upon the mossy roof, insulating it from rough weather and providing a hiding place for sparrows and their accomplices. Inside, too, the wild creatures have taken possession. A swallow's nest rests upon a rafter, whence fairy-like twitterings and whispers may be heard all through the summer. Once the fantail warblers have fledged their third brood in the neat cup nest hidden in the distant bush, they come regularly, on cool or wet days, to the shelter of the interior, prettily flirting their brown and white tails, expert at snatching up noxious flies, and, less usefully, daintily seizing spiders, which on dark days early begin to repair their silken snares under the roof and festooned along the walls.

At such times we like to sit there meditating, awaiting better weather. Young children who read Beatrix Potter and believe in fairies, but must go to bed early, sometimes invade the shed on a cool afternoon. We tell them that if they remain perfectly still, speaking only in whispers, finger to hushed lips, they may meet some of the mysterious (to them) animal characters which inhabit the old shed. There are some which live under the earth floor - hedgehog, mouse, beetle, cicada, ant . . .

They have been told - these wide-eyed, innocent young urchins - that there are other *urchins* living in the shed. We explain that the word 'urchin' is the Old English (Shakespearean) name for hedgehog. It also meant, in those days, 'goblin', hence we call the chief character 'The Goblin'. She is a hedge*sow*, a female which was rescued as an orphan, her mother having been run over on the road. The youngsters express their horror at the frequent sight of hedgehogs squashed on public roads. We tell them that a hedgehog's one weakness, and its strength, is its instinctive reaction to a threatened attack: it stops dead and rolls into a tight ball of sharp spines. No animal - cat, dog, stoat or other predator - can unroll a healthy hedgehog, but a motorcar, well . . . These casualties are mostly juvenile hedgehogs, which in late summer go awandering in search of homes of their own.

The Goblin is a stay-at-home matron. She lives deep under wood and other lumber dumped in one corner and forgotten. (The farmer says that everything comes in handy once in seven

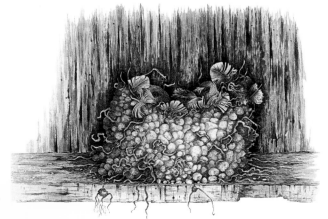

Welcome swallow nest

years.) She was unable to roll up when she was rescued, her spines soft and white. The farm children had dressed her up in doll's clothes at first, and fed her milk through a baby's dummy. Today, The Goblin is still tame enough to come to a call when her supper of meat and milk is ready, emerging from her hidden nest of leaves, twigs and chewed-up waste paper, but at four years she is middle-aged and will take no liberties from visitors. If a dog or cat tries to steal from her saucer, she nudges them away with erect prickles, ignoring their protesting whimpers. She tolerates humans out of cupboard love for the food and shelter they provide.

She is an excellent mother, defending her piglets when they are old enough to toddle after her, comically in line-ahead formation. She leads them in search of the plentiful worms which nightly emerge above the dew-wet grass to join in hermaphroditic bliss, each pair anchored by its tail in its own worm-hole. The Goblin paralyses them with swift bites; her four to six children squeal with joy as they compete for the juicy morsels. If by mischance they squeal from fear of a predator, she comes running to their defence. She has no hesitation in picking up a piglet in her mouth if it gets temporarily lost and squeals in panic after the 'crocodile' has moved on.

Hedgehogs have two, sometimes three, litters each summer. The boar takes no interest in family affairs. His main task is to patrol the home territory, ready to drive away rivals competing for the sow's favours - prickly ones, we may suppose, but the sow will lay her spines flat when ready to mate. With their keen olfactory sense they locate each other by night at the right hour of her oestrus. To test this accurate sense of smell, throw a bacon rind on the lawn, and note how your local hedgehog quickly sniffs it out with questing snout. They freely eat carrion. In their native Europe, hedgehogs will attack a small sleeping snake, grabbing it and half rolling up, impervious to striking poison fangs. In our gardens and orchards, where they feed much on slugs, snails and noxious insects and their larvae, hedgehogs are entirely beneficial.

It is popularly believed that there are two species of mice in New Zealand - the town and country sorts, but they are the same so-called house mouse, *Mus musculus*, originating in the wilderness of the southern steppes of Russia, from whence came the Celtic people to invade westwards, ultimately arriving in Britain by 500 BC. It is probable that the Celts, with their advanced knowledge of cultivating grain with the iron plough, brought *Mus musculus*, hitching a ride to Britain, hidden in a sack of seed grain. More certainly it would have been landed in cargoes of foodstuffs brought to Britain by Caesar's Roman legions. It was already a nuisance in Wales by AD 930, when the Celtic law valued a cat at fourpence - after it had caught its first mouse.

Rapid breeding when food is plentiful is the mouse's salvation. It can conceive at three months old, and have as many as ten litters of up to ten young in a year. With an assured food supply it never stops breeding. A cold store where foods are kept for long periods it finds ideal. Here, in chill semi-darkness,

your adaptable mouse lays on a thicker fur coat as it builds its nest of hessian sacking and other wrapping material. It is reported as eating its way into a frozen carcase, the rich protein diet enabling it to produce larger litters of bigger and better children. It is certainly tolerant of freezing temperatures outdoors. In summers of good seed fall of tussock and snowgrass in alpine country, it will lay up a store of seed to last the winter, snugly warm in a burrow it excavates in the ground. In such years the hardy stoat also enjoys a population increase. It puts on a white (ermine) coat and follows the mice into the high country, unfortunately for the rarer birds (takahe in Fiordland, and unique Hutton's shearwater on the Kaikoura summits), whose eggs and young are vulnerable to the mustelid.

You have to admire *Mus musculus*. An opportunist, self-introducing wherever Man has emigrated, parasitic in town or country, it can also thrive independent of Man, e.g. on small islands such as the Antipodes, where it has survived plentifully after the human colonists departed. A frenetic beast if cornered, it will attack and bite you. It is said to have been the cause of the disappearance of the kiore rat (*page 97*) thrice its size, from the evidence that when the mouse arrives, the kiore vanishes. Yet you may tame a wild mouse, as we have tamed one hungry pregnant lady nesting in the woodshed, by gentle movements when feeding scraps of food to her over quiet evening hours. We have always had an affection for Robert Burns's 'wee sleekit cow'rin, tim'rous beastie' ever since, as children, we studied the domesticated variety, multi-coloured, finger-tame friendly, which began when we were given some rejects from an experimental research medical laboratory. (The swift reproduction of this little mammal makes it ideal for research into the causes and cures of human diseases.)

Beyond the old woodshed is a large neglected orchard, intermittently grazed by a donkey, lambing sheep, a foaling mare. We like to 'perambulate at leisure' with Nature there. In winter it is visited by a lone hare which on frosty nights helps itself to cabbage or carrot in the vegetable garden. By day this hare normally crouches in its 'form', a depression in the ground or long grass, its brown shape well camouflaged until you almost tread on it, whereupon it flees with prodigious bounding leaps, kangaroo fashion. Introduced as a sporting game animal over a century ago, the European brown hare is essentially a lone, unsociable creature of wide open grassland, never taking cover in a burrow. A lame quarter-grown leveret, which we saved from the overzealous attentions of a small boy, exhibited this aloofness during its brief captivity while we fed and reared it until its lameness was cured enough to set it free. We could get no reliable information on the care of hares, but luckily remembered that the manic-depressive poet-priest, William Cowper, had written about leverets brought to him, allegedly found as orphans - mistakenly, for even as babies each leveret is deposited by the jill hare in a form separate from its siblings.

'Old Puss', who lived with Cowper nearly twelve years, and sometimes fell asleep in his lap would, wrote Cowper, 'bite the hair from my temples' as a reminder not to take liberties or to

stroke Puss. Cowper believed that God had rejected him and that he would go to Hell, but for twelve years (1774-86) his three jack hares saved his sanity. He wrote poems to them, and the best treatise on their management we know of. He recommends, and we followed, a diet of dandelion, sowthistle, lettuce, green corn, bread and other farinaceous human foods, plus milk thrice daily. He was the first to discover that the hare deliberately eats sand to aid digestion.

Unlike the sociable, stay-at-home, monogamous rabbit, the brown hare is a wandering Ishmael, never fraternising with other hares. Even the 'mad March [September in New Zealand] meetings' are boxing matches between jacks, competing for the jill's favours. Recent studies have proved that these stand-up boxing and kicking bouts, in which the jills sometimes take part, stimulate her to ovulate a few days later. She will then accept the most vigorous jack, who pursues her in a circling dance with interludes of copulatory strikes. Her oestrus over, the jill resumes her solitary existence.

Adapted to the open-air life, the jill has a longer gestation period (five weeks) than the rabbit (four weeks), but produces her four to six leverets fully furred, eyes open, and able to graze. She suckles them for a shorter period, visiting them separately until they become independent as her milk ceases to flow after about two weeks. She will produce two or more litters in a summer, but there are few records of a second mating or 'boxing match'. 'Superfoetation' occurs in the hare. The process is not fully understood, but it means, we believe, that during the early spring boxing-matches, the several copulations can result in a double pregnancy. In one horn of the uterus the embryos of the first litter develop in the normal gestation of five weeks. Meanwhile, the fertilised ova in the other uterine horn do not grow larger than pinhead size (become blastocysts is the scientific term). Their development is triggered off probably when the first litter ceases to suckle. (A similar phenomenon of carrying both a developing suckling, and a quiescent, blastocystine foetus, occurs in the female marsupial.)

In both hare and rabbit, the useful device of reabsorbing embryos occurs under stress or inadequate food supply, and overpopulation due to shortage of the same. Depending on how severe this stress is, the embryos die off in the womb, one by one, until only a few - or none - survive. There is no abortion: each embryo shrivels in turn and becomes reabsorbed into the mother's bloodstream. (Really a neat form of birth control, if only the secret of the physical trigger of this device could be found, and applied to the unwanted human pregnancy!)

The hare possesses one of the largest hearts, in proportion to its size, in the animal world. It needs this huge athlete's heart, for a vast quantity of blood must be pumped through it when a hare is escaping its enemies by prodigous leaping and long-distance, cross-country marathons.

The rabbit has a normal (small) heart, for it never runs farther than back to its underground warren when danger threatens. Every warren has several exits and entrances. When predatory stoat, ferret or weasel enters, the occupants can rapidly exit, or, if they fear predators outside as well, they will dodge through other passages below ground. In the last resort - as any rabbit ferreter will tell you - the experienced rabbit squats with its head thrust into the earth at the blind end of an underground tunnel, presenting only its rump to the predator's fangs, which may well fail to obtain a strong enough hold on fur and skin to drag the victim out and deliver a lethal bite on the head. (Mustelids are notoriously impatient, and will retire with nothing more than jaws and claws full of fur.)

Observe, on sunny afternoons when rabbits first appear to graze, how sociable the family is. The dominant adult buck in a warren will preen and lick his doe's face, ears and fur as she relaxes sleepily in the sun. The rabbit kittens play around her, and father tolerates them when they try to include him in their games. At the same time he is watchful of the movements of other adults in sight. He will ignore another grown female, but will run at and drive away a full-grown buck which dares to trespass on the plot of grazing around his warren, his territory

which from time to time he patrols. In the breeding season from early spring to midsummer, he marks his property by depositing scent from a gland under his chin, rubbed against the boundaries, and upon his family. The grazing limits are also defined by a series of 'lavatories' - heaped faecal pellets, identifiable by their individual and sexual scent. At times an aggressive, unmated buck will approach and 'try out' the resident 'king' buck. In the ensuing fight their scrabbling forepaws and kicking hind claws occasionally inflict bloody wounds, but mostly it is a show of force. Possession is a nine-tenths of rabbit law, and an indignant 'king' can humiliate a rival by a well-aimed squirt of strong-smelling urine. The rabbit lives much in the world of scent-recognition, natural to a life of nocturnal activity and dwelling below ground.

Long domesticated from its wild European ancestor the polecat, the ferret, *Mustela putorius*, was introduced about 100 years ago for the purpose of controlling rabbit plagues. In this it failed, although it does hunt rabbits and rats through their burrows. It is also a fierce predator of ground-living birds. Unlike the stoat it is not a tree-climber and prefers swampy ground where it feeds on frogs, fish and any small wildlife it can find with its keen sense of smell and hearing.

The doe instinctively hides her litter of up to ten kittens, born naked and blind, in an underground 'stop' which she digs secretly away from the warren. She works with astonishing speed on the day of her parturition, lining the hole with grass and an inner blanket of her own fur, stripped from her belly, thus exposing her teats. She covers up the stop with earth and grass so cunningly smoothed over it is difficult to detect. She opens it once a night to suckle the kittens. They are well furred when at about ten days of age they push their way to the surface, needing more air. They will be independent at a month old, just before the doe digs another stop for her next litter. She mates within a day or so of her last parturition, and is more or less continuously pregnant until midsummer. The moult now begins and there is a 'neutral' period of about three months when the buck's libido ceases, when old and young mingle freely and harmoniously. The juveniles, wandering far, meeting other young rabbits, are playing at sweethearts in preparation for their first partnership in starting a new home and family.

Around the old orchard numerous butterflies flutter among the weeds and wildflowers. A native of North America the splendid black, white and gold monarch butterfly, *Danaus plexippus*, island-hopped across the Pacific to Australia and New Zealand about a century ago, no doubt aided by the traffic of ships and artificially by persons happy to have such an attractive insect in a land of few native butterfly species. Its main food plant is the introduced swan plant, *Asclepias fruticosa*, today grown in many gardens to encourage this lovely butterfly.

It flaunts its beauty in bold flights in the sun, fearless of attack by birds. To them its conspicuous colours are a warning. During the caterpillar stage of feeding on the toxic swan plant, it accumulates cardenolites (heart poison) in its body tissues,

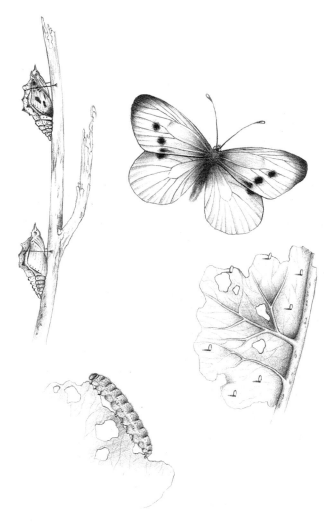

Life cycle of the white butterfly

which causes vomiting and severe distress if swallowed. Nevertheless the shining cuckoo and certain shield bugs and wasps are recorded as feeding on monarch larvae.

There are several generations in summer, the last of which over-winters in semi-hibernation, clustering in certain favourite evergreen trees in sheltered sites. In the spring the male emits his sexual scent from a tiny pocket in each hind wing to lure a female to mate. She glues her tiny conical white eggs singly to swan plant leaves, on which the strikingly marked caterpillars feed so voraciously as often to devour all the leaves and much of the stems. When this threatens we like to transfer a few full-fed larvae to alternative food plants, by placing a branch of a pepper tree or the so-called moth-catching plant, *Arauljia sericofera*, in water under the house eaves. As soon as they cease feeding, the larvae crawl to the dry shelter of the eaves where they attach and spin their bell-like silk cocoons.

The cabbage white butterfly, *Pieris rapae*, today everywhere numerous and widespread in temperate climates, came to us from the Old World. It is a strong migrant under pressure of population. It reached Canada about 1860, Mexico by 1880, whence it crossed to Hawaii by 1889. Probably assisted by imports of fruit and vegetables, it was recorded at Napier in 1930. A few years later 'millions were seen flying in all directions from Napier'. It became impossible to raise marketable brassica crops on the commercial scale for which Hawke's Bay was famous at that time; cabbage leaves were reduced to skeletons by successive rapid generations of *P. rapae* each summer.

In its native Europe this butterfly is kept in check by its natural parasites. As an early example of biological warfare one of these, the ichneumon wasp, *Apanteles glomeratus*, was successfully introduced. This little wasp glues its eggs upon the young caterpillar. The grub quickly hatches and enters the body of its host, feeding at first on the non-vital tissues. Later, when the parasitised caterpillar ceases to eat and crawls feebly to a dry place where a healthy caterpillar normally pupates, the larval wasps devour their host's vital organs and themselves pupate. They emerge from the shrivelled caterpillar skin to spin their own golden-coloured cocoons alongside in the same dry situation. Another introduced ichneumon takes a short cut: the minute *Pteromalus puparium* searches for a healthy cabbage-white chrysalis upon which she glues her eggs. The grubs enter and devour the inert body of the developing butterfly.

Thus the plague of these butterflies has been reduced to much less harmful proportions, although commercial growers of quality brassica crops still consider it necessary to protect these by insecticide spraying. This butterfly instinctively seeks cabbage and other strongly scented plants rich in mustard oils on which to lay its eggs, including nasturtium, mignonette and cleome. Despite the apparently feeble wavering flight of those we see in our gardens, it has been proved that the cabbage white travels long distances. We have frequently watched them migrating from one island to another, even drifting far over the open sea. They seem very restless; those individuals we see in our garden one day are probably not the same we see on the next day.

Where ragwort and groundsel grow freely a day-flying moth is commonly seen, especially in the mornings and evenings. The handsome magpie moth, *Nyctemera annulata*, black winged with pale yellow spots, attaches its shining golden eggs beneath the leaves of *Senecio* species, including the related garden cineraria and native rangiora. The eggs rapidly darken, giving birth to the well-known 'woolly bear' caterpillars, reddish black and sprouting long black hairs from each of a dozen segments. With increasing appetite they will completely defoliate each small food plant then march on to the next. Because of its dark colour, hairiness and apparent unpalatability, this caterpillar is avoided by most birds. However it is assiduously sought and devoured by the migrant New Zealand shining cuckoo during that visitor's summer sojourn. Not always with a profitable result - one morning a neighbour's cat emerged from our large clump of cinerarias with a shining cuckoo in its jaws!

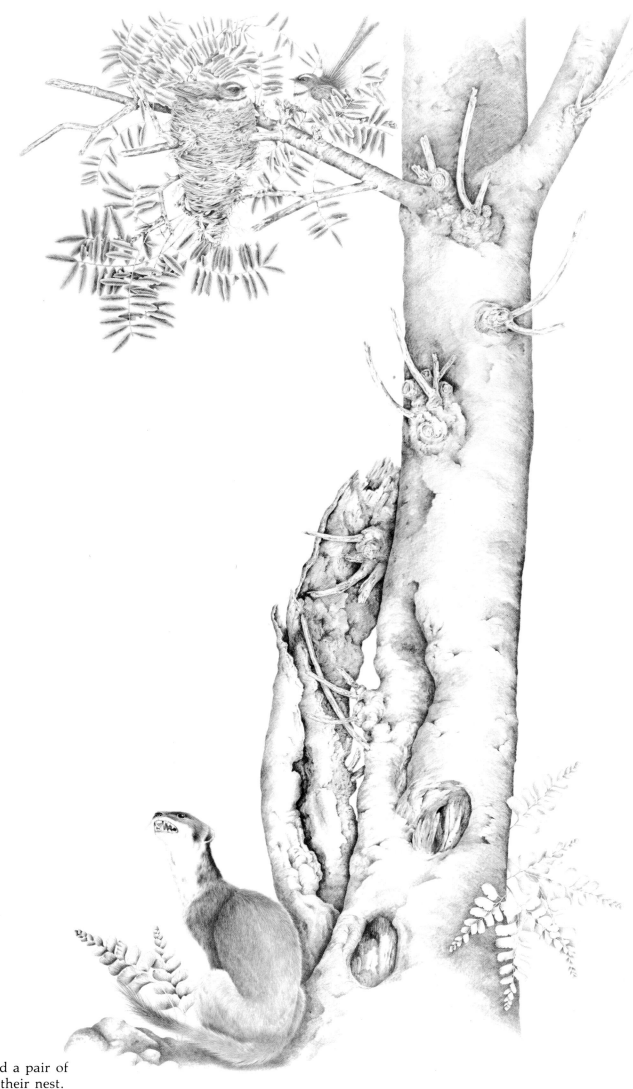

A stoat has detected a pair of
fantail warblers at their nest.

Paddock and Bush

God made the country, and man made the town.
William Cowper (1731-1800)

A sunlit early spring day on the farm. It is delightful to admire and study the natural and human activity in a typical paddock in process of cultivation. The double or triple mouldboard of the tractor plough opens the secret treasury of small life below ground, swiftly rolling over each continuous 'slice' of moist soil to fall smoothly into the preceding furrow. Gulls are fearless in competition to pounce upon the squirming creatures thus exposed - the large fat earthworms, the innumerable grubs and pupae of root-eating cicadas, crickets, craneflies, beetles and moths. In long-established pasture larger nocturnal animals may be uplifted by the plough - a lizard or a gecko, at times a mouse rudely ejected from its ball nest of dry grass and store of gathered seeds.

Over-eager red-billed and black-billed gulls, smaller and less dominant than the arrogant black-backs, on occasion plunge upon a juicy item revealed between two falling furrow slices, which may fold up on and trap a gull's thrusting head. Unless the ploughman notices the struggling bird and stops to release it, it is in danger of being strangled by the time the tractor returns to plough the next furrow. Gone are the leisurely days of the horse-drawn plough, with the ploughman walking behind the turning furrow. The modern operator sits comfortably ahead of the plough, which is moving at much greater speed, and such wildlife casualties may be ploughed under, recycled to nourish the earth.

Starlings are almost as bold, but more nimble to escape as they run eagerly behind the gulls to snatch up smaller prizes, their spear bills extracting wireworm (larvae of the click beetle), leatherjacket (larvae of the cranefly or daddy-long-legs), or, a major pest, the native scarab beetle, known to the Maori as tutaeruru, which has a voracious appetite for pasture. All these insects are natural inhabitants of the undisturbed wild grassland of New Zealand, their numbers controlled by native parasites and predators. But with the intensive large-scale farming of land for crops and pasture, two blades where one grew before, these undercover graziers moved in to the paddocks well ahead of their natural enemies of the undeveloped and bush country.

The Pakeha colonists of the last century found their first crops so heavily attacked by the native grass grub, *Costelytra zealandica,* that at times infested pasture became a brown dying carpet which, when ploughed open, exposed thousands of fat white grubs to the square metre. Sparrows were imported mistakenly to control this plague, but being seed-eaters, preferred to devour the ripening grain. However, the importation of insectivorous starlings proved highly beneficial and to this day farmers welcome starlings enough to set up nest-boxes for them on their properties. Orchardists are less happy when starlings claim their wages in ripe fruit.

After the winter rains the moist paddock soil yields easily to the plough, and the harvest of worms and grubs is greedily devoured by the starlings; they are opportunely laying up fat for the approaching summer activities after leaner winter months. We note that at this season about 50 per cent are young birds born some nine months earlier - which is approximately the spring-time ratio of young to adult population in most bird species. These adolescents are still wearing the dull brown, immature plumage. This lacks the irridescent shine of the adult coat, which is handsomely spangled with white polka dots. They are not yet paired. Some will spend the burgeoning spring weeks in 'sweethearting', as it has been called, adjusting to young birds of the opposite sex, and eventually settling in a neighbourhood of grassland habitat where food is plentiful enough for the raising of their first family. Depending on competition from the established pairs, it may take more than a year before the young birds are settled and successful, usually within a few kilometres of their birthplace. In spring their once-loving parents will drive them from the vicinity of the nest in which they were born, but as in the human predicament, there is a deep-seated nostalgia or instinct to return to the well-remembered place where they first enjoyed the security of loving care, food and protection. Starlings are as property conscious, homeloving and clannish as we are.

Meanwhile observe how the established pair behave differently. The male, after each bout of filling his crop with ploughshare food, flies to some nearby conspicuous perch. Here he utters his happy song, a wheezy medley which often includes mimicking the calls of pukeko, pheasant, quail, sparrow, tui, even the wolf-whistle of a passing human youth. Certainly he sounds cheerful, but his song is also his advertisement of his

Female starling feeding young

dominance to other starlings who might challenge his position in the neighbourhood hierarchy. More than likely his mate is within earshot, and presently will fly to his side. They exchange squawks of recognition. In such birds where the sexes are so much alike externally, mate-recognition is mainly by voice. Yet, close to, in this early spring and late winter month, there are slight colour differences visible, the iridescent plumage of the female is more spangled with the white polka dots than that of her mate. And nearer still you will discover that the eye, uniform brown in the male, has a distinct pale white or golden ring in the female.

41

Starling eggs

Hard frost and snow inland drive the winter flocks to the mild coastline where starlings gather at sunset to roost in thousands in dense plantations and cliffside vegetation, even in caves, especially on small islands where they are safe from prowling cats and stoats. It is the experienced adults, dressed in their spangled winter finery, which remember these safe sites and guide the brown juveniles to the roost. Except when nesting, starlings are intensely sociable and like to spend idle moments perched on roofs or treetops in close groups, peacefully preening and chattering.

Already our cock starling singing on the bare bough is losing his polka dots; these are really the buffish-white tips to new feathers, and wear away without the rest of the feather being moulted, making the summer plumage darker and more iridescent. In a few more weeks he will be investigating a nest-box or hole in the eaves. He will start building or rebuilding the nest alone. He will pause outside with a mouthful of grass and leaves, calling to his mate, as if he would remind her of her duty, but although she will inspect the work at intervals, not until she is about to lay her clutch of six or more eggs will she take charge and add the furniture - feathers, twigs, dry moss. She seems fussy about this, and works on her own. The pale eggs (like most eggs laid in a dark place, paleness makes them easier to see) are beautiful as jewels, glossy and washed a delicate blue-green, when you occasionally find one on your lawn. This is the not-infrequent misfortune of an inexperienced, perhaps nestless young hen.

Introduced birds feeding freely in paddocks include the Californian quail with its decorative top-knot more prominent in the male (top); the English rook; the white-backed magpie; the Indian myna; and the spur-winged plover of Australia - all largely feeders on insects with seeds in the autumn.

The handsome pheasant from Asia.

Some males have a pretty habit of presenting a plucked flower to their incubating hens. She sits tight as soon as the last egg is laid, but encourages her mate to take her place during the day at intervals when she needs exercise and food. Both assiduously bring live insects, caterpillars, worms, weevils, etc. to feed the clamorous brood. In three weeks they leave their nest, and are led by their parents to fill their crops with the first summer berries. On our Northland coast the abundant dark berries of the early-flowering *Osteospermum* or golden daisy shrub are popular. Later when the flax is in flower, starlings copy the tui and bellbird and dip their bills into the cups of nectar.

Since there were no enclosed paddocks before the arrival of the Pakeha colonist less than two centuries ago, there are no strictly endemic (New Zealand evolved) birds adapted to survival in this man-made open habitat. The noble-looking harrier (bush hawk) just now soaring above the busy tractor, no doubt with its binocular vision focused on animal food emerging from the upturned soil, is a self-introduced immigrant from Australia.

There are other 'exotic' birds attracted to the paddock. When the tractor is silent while the driver takes a smoko, we hear the sharp call of the handsome peach and blue *Halcyon sancta*, the sacred kingfisher common throughout Australasia. With luck we have heard and encountered the large kookaburra, the Australian 'laughing jackass' kingfisher, originally released on Kawau Island, Northland, but it remains scarce.

43

There are several European finches. A cock yellowhammer stammers his 'bread and butter and no chee-eese' song from his high perch on a macrocarpa. Mixed parties of goldfinches, red-polls, and greenfinches feed amicably together where the banks of thistles and other arable land weeds are seeding close to the fence. They are as much at home in weedy paddocks as in their European habitat with nesting cover in gardens and bush nearby.

Cut-over native bush borders two sides of this paddock. The amateur naturalist enjoys a quiet prowl along its perimeter, stopping to peer and probe its natural secrets, its mixture of native and introduced plants and animals. We poke our stick into a hollow puriri tree, felled many years ago. Sometimes an opossum will be sleeping there. Out peeps a gecko, dozy enough to be captured under our handkerchief. It proves to be the fairly common *Hoplodactylus pacificus* of the North Island.

The midday sun burns down on this borderland of paddock and bush, shining on a battlefield of plant species contending for light and space to survive. It is dominated by aggressive imported grasses, blackberry, gorse, hawthorn, privet, wattle, alien honeysuckle and ragwort, according to the nature of its soil and climate, and the amount of human interference. Man's continuing assault on natural woodland by felling and burning has made the deteriorated bush a reservoir for the introduced species.

Ragwort is said to be poisonous to farm stock if eaten fresh in quantity - though harmless when withered in hay. Honey bees which eagerly collect pollen and nectar from ragwort produce honey which is unpalatable and unsaleable on the market. How poisonous are the several other native and imported *Senecio* species ranging over the whole of New Zealand? Many of them are handsome enough to be popular as flowering shrubs in the garden.

We pull up another so-called poisonous common weed of disturbed soil, the black nightshade, *Solanum nigrum*; it has purplish pointed leaves and bright yellow and purple blossom, like that of its cousin, the potato, *S.tuberosum*. We reflect that to drink the leaf sap of either is to die a Socrates death. Yet - how strange - there is a beetle whose grub feeds exclusively on green potato leaves, devouring them as avidly as the woolly-bear caterpillar consumes ragwort. The Colorado or *doryphore* beetle is much hated by potato growers for defoliating their crops; fortunately so far it has been kept out of New Zealand.

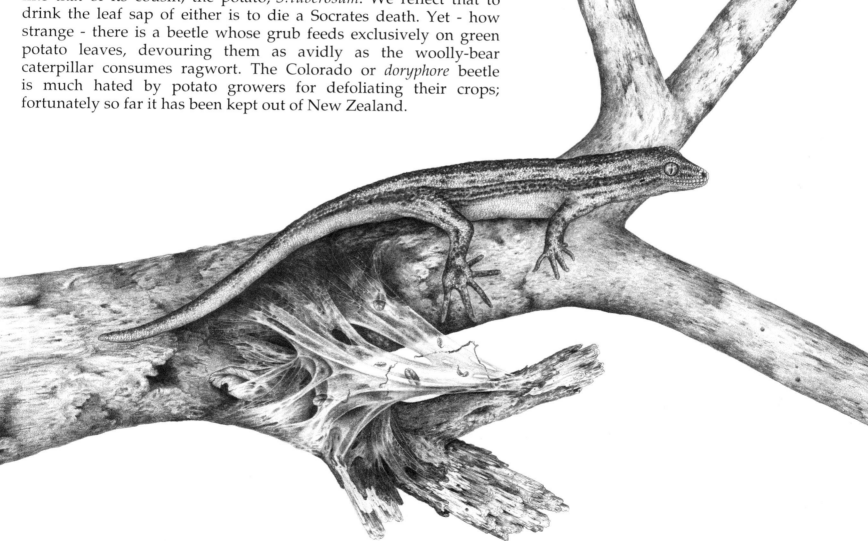

Hoplodactylus pacificus, the common gecko.

45

The yellow admiral butterfly, *Bassaris itea* is both a resident and wandering migrant between Australia and New Zealand. Its hairy caterpillar feeds on nettle leaves, cleverly constructing a hiding 'tent' by pulling leaves together with silken twine. This does not protect the helpless newly-moulted chrysalis from the attacks of the large introduced ichneumon wasp, *Eththromorpha intricatoria*. This red-legged parasite also lays its single egg on the pupa of the common red admiral butterfly, *B. gonerlilla*, another nettle feeder. The wasp pierces the tender skin with its ovipositor, but if the skin has already hardened the ichneumon is no longer interested. It is worth growing a patch of nettles in a corner of your garden to attract these handsome butterflies.

The name 'solanum' is derived from 'comforting', referring to the use of solanum essence in pain-killing drugs. The large, sparse leaves of *Solanum mauritianum*, the woody flannelweed shrub, naturalised along the New Zealand shore, cause a mild rash on sensitive human skins when brushed against, for which reason some people attempt to eradicate it. But it is not without merit and a place in the littoral ecology. It grows rapidly, but never beyond shrub size, and dies back after a few years. It provides filtered shade for young native trees we have planted in coastal reserves. Its typical solanum blossom is pretty and its multi-coloured berries are eaten by birds, silver-eyes especially.

As a young man I collected herbs, lichens and toadstools to supply a herbalist's city emporium. At that teenage period I planned enthusiastically to become a herb farmer. I learned of the healing, narcotic and lethal virtues of certain plants, from which extracts were made to cure human disorders. Even the vile-smelling hemlock, belladonna (deadly nightshade), bittersweet, henbane and thorn-apple had their uses as 'tinctures' in therapeutic medicines I was told, just as the skunk's stinking anal fluid is today used to strengthen the aromatic base of modern cosmetic productions.

Stinging nettles, *Urtica*, have many useful properties; they exceed spinach as a source of iron when lightly boiled or made into a pudding or porridge with other ingredients. The venom is dissipated by heat. And there are recipes for tasty nettle wine, beer and tea. I learned that you should not swallow the milky juice of spurges, *Euphorbia,* but this freshly applied from the cut stem of the common annual, *E. peplis,* in our garden, caused warts on my hand to vanish. Almost all the common weeds of cultivation are listed today in modern books (for example, see A.W.Hatfield's *How to Enjoy your Weeds* dealing with the now popular back-to-nature or 'naturist' use of herbs for medicinal and culinary purposes). There are recipes to relieve all human 'aches, pains, boils and blanes' by concoctions (especially of tea made from the leaves) of chickweed, dandelion, coltsfoot, groundsel, couch grass, ground ivy, potentilla, etc.

One of our favourite herbs is the common yarrow of the wayside, *Achillea millefolium,* a vigorous perennial found world-wide in temperate lands. We have seen it flourishing outside the met. station on the remote, chill Campbell Islands, farthest south of New Zealand lands. Yarrow was named after Achilles, who staunched his wounds with this herb. Far back in antiquity it was esteemed for its power of healing mental stress, and soothing the brain for meditation. According to Chinese philosophy older than Christianity (see *The I-Ching Book of Oracles*) you have only to hold fresh yarrow in your hand to attain rebirth of the spirit. Today as we plucked a tender young shoot with its crown of fine leaves, we felt a nostalgic pleasure in remembering its discovery and aromatic scent as children. For us it seemed to renew once more the wildflowers' message of healing nature - that the earth, despite man's arrogant misuse of the planet's resources, will remain.

Poisonous *Amanita* toadstools with manuka flowers and seed capsules.

47

Native Forest

*And there were forests ancient as the hills
Enfolding sunny spots of greenery.*
S.T.Coleridge (1772-1834)

There is no wooded country in the world, of the many we have visited, more beautiful to walk in than the mature native forests of New Zealand, for centuries unravished by axe or fire. Alas, they are pitifully few today, and the more precious thereby. Those which survive have done so by the accident of their remote situation, protected by high, steep mountainous land far from road access and with a heavy rainfall to keep them green and safe from fire. Their beauty lies in the variety of unique tall trees of ancient lineage which share the high canopy. They are evergreen, shedding their sparse narrow leaves throughout the year. There is light, shade, moisture and humus for a rich fauna and flora at all levels below. As species unique to our land, these giants evolved from more primitive forms many millions of years ago in Gondwanaland centuries. Today they are known by names given by the Maori, first settlers to see the forests of Aotearoa barely a thousand years ago: kauri, rimu, tawa, matai, miro, totara, kowhai and kahikatea. (This last is our tallest rain forest tree - up to 65 m.)

Evolving in a mammal-less land with few bees and butterflies, these trees became dependent largely on birds for the fertilisation of their seed and its dispersal. Tui, bellbird, native parrots, stitchbird and similar smaller native birds drank their nectar and transferred their pollen from flower to flower. Their seeds, often contained within a succulent coloured berry eagerly devoured by birds, passed through the avian digestive system unscathed, to be dropped at random in a capsule of faeces - the last an advantage aiding regeneration.

Longest-lived is the kauri, *Agathis australis*, a cone-bearing giant once widespread but now confined to the northern half of the North Island. The famous Tane Mahuta kauri in Waipoua Forest is believed to be over 2000 years old, but its height at 51 m is now declining, its heart-wood hollow and rotting. Slow to grow, kauri is also slow to die. Under centuries of humus deposition its roots are mingled with hardened resinous gum exuded as sap high up in the bark. After centuries of slow decay each huge forest tree must one day be toppled or split open by the occasional typhonic gale. When in 1973 the legendary giant kauri, Kope, collapsed, a large colony of native short-tailed bats was discovered in its hollow heart. Kope's demise was a perfectly

OPPOSITE: Tui and nectar-rich kowhai blossom.

Kauri *Agathis australis* of
Northland native forests.

natural event and some 500 bats were quick to transfer to
another hollow kauri, the ancient Whakamakere; this was felled
by a cyclone in 1975. Scientists were able to study this native bat,
Mystacina tuberculata, as a consequence. Its habits and
appearance are unique in the bat world. Although it catches
insects on the wing at night, it also crawls on the ground, on
trees and among foliage. Its stomach contents were found to
contain remains of tree fruits, pollen and the nectar of flowers.
Its long tongue has an unusual brush of fine papillae or taste
buds for extracting nectar. On Little Barrier Island one evening
we watched this little bat crawling actively over boulder-strewn
ground in search of hoppers and other nocturnal insects. Its
membranous wings were so folded that the supporting four
'fingers' formed a firm prop or crutch as it moved forward
agilely, assisted by the strong clawed feet. In this situation it was

plain to us that its very short tail, which has hardly any webbing, was an advantage. The only other bat in New Zealand is the strictly aerial hunter *Chalinolobus tuberculatus*, an Australian species which has a long tail supporting a large femoral web between its legs which, as in many other bat species, is used as a basket to hold its winged captures momentarily.

The death fall of any of the forest giants opens more sunlight and living space for the plants and animals of the lower canopy or understorey, and the forest floor itself. In these 'sunny spots of greenery' dormant seeds of the old tree shoot forth; a few of the strongest will survive to replace the parent species.

A century ago the mouldering, prostrate giant was a food store for some now extinct endemic birds. The handsome huia ripped open bark, already rotten with fungi, with its powerful curved bill and extracted the large grubs of the huhu beetle and other boring insects; native thrush, saddleback and bush wren probed the forest floor debris for the smaller insects and larvae. There have never been any true woodpeckers in New Zealand, but this lack is supplied today by the kaka parrot, still found in most native forests. With its powerful, hooked beak the kaka can strip away the bark of living trees attacked by borer grubs.

Kaka

The understorey of the native forest forms a canopy of smaller endemic trees rising to about half the height of the top layer. These are mostly berry-bearing hardwoods or broadleafs, mingled with the tall tree ferns for which New Zealand is justly famous. There are climbing plants (lianes) ascending the middle canopy; a few reach the sunlight of the roof. Their list is long: sweet-scented native jasmine, honeysuckle and passionfruit; wiry muehlenbeckia; rope-like cables of scarlet-flowering rata; the showy clematis *C. paniculata*, which has white rata-like flowers, and the yellow *C. foetida*; the twining mattress-like mangemange fern *Lygodium articulatum*, and the smooth, black, tough fretwork of the supplejack *Rhipogonum scandens*, sometimes obstructive of human progress through the forest.

The unravished native forest is a fairyland of filtered light glancing through the cathedral columns of tall trees. At ground level we tread on ferns and minute orchids thriving under gentle shade and soft light. The moist air and accumulations of humus and moss upon a niche or crotch of a tree encourage the epiphyte spore or seed to germinate. *Griselinia lucida* (the Maori puka) shoots first as a perching epiphyte, from which it grows descending arms to reach and root into the ground; these develop into thick cables resembling the limbs of the supporting tree. Filmy ferns, climbing ferns, moss, club-moss and liverworts decorate the flanks of giant trees; the curious, primitive stiff-leaved *Tmesipteris tannensis* chooses to climb the spiky trunk of tall tree ferns.

Walking in the Bay of Plenty's Rotoehu Forest one fine morning in search of the rare kokako, we paused where a decaying totara log lay in a sunny space made by its fall. Moss, fungi and liverwort made it difficult to find a dry place to sit, but when we did attempt to, our weight caused the rotted timber to collapse, and we, ignominiously, with it. The next half hour produced an interesting sequence of events.

Our companion was an entomologist, and immediately began collecting the abundant insects revealed by the accident, the numerous fauna of rotten pulp and bark: woodlice, beetle and weevil adults and larvae, spring-tails, hoppers, worms, wetas, and - what he prized most - a peripatus or 'walking worm'. As he rooted through the debris he pointed out to us that the peripatus, along with the centipedes, several spiders and certain carnivorous beetles, had been preying on the vegetarian wood pulp and fungi feeders.

Meanwhile a pair of fantails had arrived and were dancing hither and thither, snatching up the exposed insect life at our feet, now and then flitting off to swallow a mouthful at leisure on a branch close by. Suddenly there was a hiss of wings as a falcon swooped, seemingly out of thin air, and carried off one fantail in non-stop flight. New Zealand's only falcon hunts by this high-speed dash, a mixture of the (European) sparrow-hawk's surprise swerving in and out of cover and the peregrine falcon's bolt-like launching upon its prey. Our falcon is just as fierce and fast, and moreover is normally unafraid of man, save where, as in the past, it was persecuted for killing poultry and game.

OPPOSITE: The native falcon on nest.

A few fantail feathers floated down as the falcon passed overhead, its prey crushed in its rapier talons, momentarily circling and screaming its annoyance at discovering us below. Faintly in response we heard an answering 'hek-hek-hek' repeated at intervals - its partner was somewhere near. That repeated 'hekking' cry is typical of the falcon alarmed for the safety of its nest. Following in the direction of the sound, within a few minutes we were guided through low forest covering a stony ravine. Circling over her nest on a bare rock ledge, the splendid, somewhat larger and darker female falcon screamed her displeasure as long as we remained near - which was not for very long, for both birds dive-bombed us very close at times, a somewhat nerve-wracking experience. Our caps were pulled tightly about our heads, just in case of a direct hit!

Rotoehu Forest is but a remnant of the northern limit of the once vast central North Island native forests which spread south to the great lake of Taupo and into the eastern wilderness of the Urewera. A huge area - the Kaingaroa - is now under radiata pine, providing a valuable timber industry and supplying paper and pulp mills. But in pockets of native forest, in steep gorges too difficult to log, we have found the rare, shy kokako. These are relict, declining populations of this beautiful bird, once common throughout native forests, but today limited to those of the northern half of the North Island.

Named by the Maori from its 'ko-ka-ko' call, the native crow has a harsh repertoire of twanging notes. We have been able to attract this handsome blue-wattled bird into view by playing a tape-recording of its vocalisations while hiding in cover in the forest. It is estimated that this territorial bird requires possibly 2000 hectares of endemic forest for a viable colony of several pairs to exist - and this forest must be continuous, not in separated parcels. The kokako's natural habitat is largely the understorey, for it is a poor performer on the wing - in fact it is on its way to becoming flightless. It prefers to climb and leap through the understorey where it feeds almost exclusively on leaves, flowers and berries. (These are also fed to the young.) By this means it is able to climb to the forest roof. It can glide downwards on its rounded wings, but will not cross a large open space if this means descending to the ground.

As twilight falls the plump, glossy native pigeons wing clatteringly to roost in the canopy. They have fed the day long on almost every species of wild fruit, or on flowers and tender leaves. Unlike the kokako, this bold bird walks freely on the ground, and like its smaller cousin, the European wood pigeon, will gobble up young clover. It is especially fond of kowhai blossom, as we well remember from its raids on our garden, where it also seeks out laburnum and broom flowers.

Early at dusk the morepork owl calls from near its day roost in thicket or nest-hole, as if warning the small prey it will be hunting on silent wing. In reality it is a signal to its mate or any other morepork that it is 'on station' - its established hunting territory. The little forest birds - tomtit, yellowhead, rifleman, silver-eye, fantail and grey warbler - have long retired within thick leafy cover to sleep off bellies full of forest insects.

OPPOSITE: Kokako at nest with young.

Berry foods of the native pigeon (from top): miro, tawa, karamu, taraire, pigeonwood. Since it has been fully protected the native pigeon has increased and is now found in some larger suburban parks and reserves close to cities. The Maori know it as kereru.

Just before it is too dark for human eyes to see them against the night sky, native bats emerge from hollows in trees and rocks. If your ears are sharp you may catch their normal 'keep in touch' squeaks to each other, but not the higher ultrasonic calls they broadcast to locate their aerial prey by the echoes received back by the sonar computer in the bat brain - by which they accurately measure the distance and direction of moth or other winged insect food.

Stand still to hear other more audible sounds of the forest night. Scraping on trees is likely to come from the ugly-looking wetas. They also make clicking noises by rubbing their spiny legs together. Although fearsome in appearance they are largely vegetarian, eating bark and foliage; they only bite in self-defence if you handle them. They hide by day in crevices in trees or the ground. They have many enemies: owls, hawks, rats, mice, wild pigs, and night-prowling weka and kiwi. There are many species, including some giants evolved on off-shore islands.

During the midnight hours there is increased activity in the humus layer, the habitat of the large, handsome endemic forest snails. In Nelson area national parks we have found *Paryphanta* and *Powelliphanta* spp. up to 8cm across the coiled shell. Unlike the spirally twisted vegetarian flax snails, these flat coiled species of the deep forest are carnivorous, slithering through the carpet of dead leaves in search of the humus-eating worms.

This is the domain of the kiwi, New Zealand's national bird. No doubt it is qualified for this role by its uniqueness, but character-wise the kiwi has many good points. The male is the perfect stay-at-home husband, taking on the whole duty of incubation. It is still fairly common in large forests and some have returned to cut-over bush which is regenerating. The kiwi probes the soft ground for worms and grubs, locating these principally by smell – its nostrils are uniquely placed at the tip of the long bill. It has poor eyesight, but keen hearing. If you remain perfectly still on hearing the snuffling noises of a kiwi blowing its nose to clear its nostrils after a bout of delving, it may well ignore you as it blunders past, its cat-like whiskers helping it to avoid obstacles along its nightly path. It will sniff out (or hear) any insect or larvae it can seize; in season it eats ripe berries fallen from trees. Its stomach usually contains grit - swallowed to aid digestion, perhaps?

56

North Island kiwi *Apteryx australis*

As a large, plump bird the kiwi was much prized for food by the Maori, who hunted it with the help of the kuri, the now-extinct Maori dog. It is now strictly protected by law, and believed to be maintaining its numbers. Some farmers about to clear bush known to harbour kiwis have helpfully asked naturalists to organise their removal to other forests often lacking these birds. In helping to round up these kiwis, we have learned one way not to handle a kiwi. Do not grab or hold one except by both legs! For a small bird the kiwi has an almighty kick which inflicts a nasty wound on your unguarded hand. Its huge feet are armed with sharp claws. We believe it is this kicking method of defence that has enabled the kiwi to keep the introduced mustelid predators at bay - ferret, stoat, weasel - so lethal to other hole-nesting, flightless, or weak-winged birds such as the laughing owl, kakapo, huia and saddleback, now extinct on the mainland.

OVER PAGE: Morepork owls and prey.

Sika deer head, antlers not yet
fully developed.

OPPOSITE: The handsome but
unwelcome opossum

Unfortunately these and other mammals introduced by
white settlers increasingly penetrate the remaining endemic
forest. Often they enter these the more easily by way of new
paths opened up by foresters, trampers and hunters. Wild
animals of any size find these tracks unobstructed highways for
exploration and the natural dispersal of their young at the close
of the breeding season.

Introduced deer, which are natural browsers of forest,
increased to such an extent in areas where it was difficult to hunt
them - as in Fiordland forests - that they denuded the humus
floor of regenerating trees. At the moment with the strong
demand for venison and for stock for deer farming ventures,
wild deer populations are being reduced. Helicopters are
employed to achieve this, with marksmen using nets and
tranquilliser guns.

The introduction of the Australian opossum, *Trichosurus vulpecula*, as a producer of fur from our native forests was another folly. It cannot be hunted by day, when it sleeps secure in forest cover - secure also from natural enemies, for there are no climbing predators powerful enough to kill this substantial browser of tender foliage. Although its rate of reproduction seems slow (usually one, rarely two young annually to a mature female) it is still spreading over the whole of New Zealand. Surplus opossums from the forests colonise even city gardens and orchards, where they devour cultivated fruit and flowers.

The worst aspect of the present method of opossum control is not only the failure to check the increase, but the popular and legalised use of poison baits and steel-jawed traps in native forests. Our rarer endemic birds die even more easily than opossums by sniffing or tasting cyanide poison or blundering into these inhumane traps. There are many one-legged kiwis today found in native forests subject to opossum control; a one-legged bird has no hope of breeding, even should it survive. One fact is clear. We shall never exterminate opossum, stoat, ferret, cat and other long established mammal pests in this country. We have to live with them as part of our natural scene today, but it should not be beyond the skill of Man to devise more humane methods of control.

The fearsome-looking weta is vegetarian.

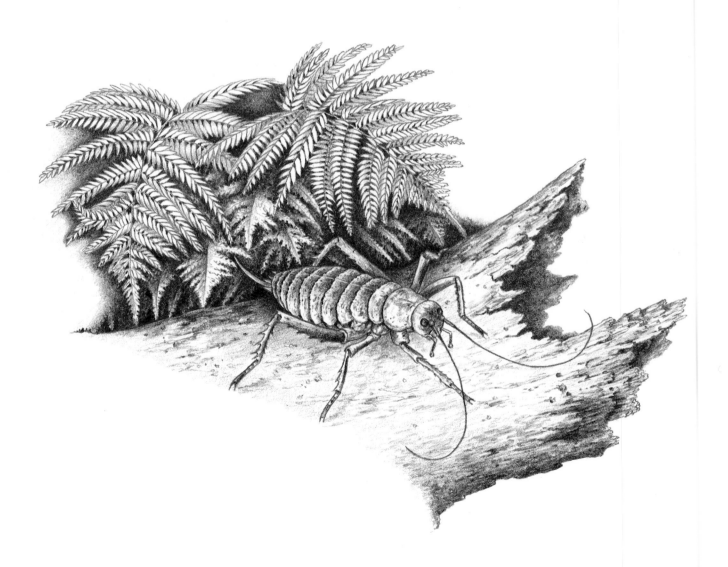

Exotic Forest

Forestry is conservation.
New Zealand Forest Service

Naturalists look for and may find beauty even in plantations of exotic conifer, eucalypt and other man-made forests, the huge and growing extent of which is often decried by some environmentalists, who object to the clearance of our remnant native forests for commercial production of alien trees. However, in terms of employment, and the need for timber for building and export, these fast-growing plantations have become a valuable renewable resource in the national economy. Although our endemic species yield durable timber of pleasing colour and 'grain' for building purposes of all sorts they are notably slow to reach maturity and are rarely planted commercially today. Early in the present century it was proved that, grown in our favourable soil and damp climate, certain exotic species mature at least twice as fast as the majority of our natives.

Most notable of these exotics was the Monterey pine, *Pinus radiata*, a native of California. By continuously selecting for seed those pines which grew quickly, free of disease, and of good shape - straight and tall - for timber, foresters have developed radiata strains fit to be felled as marketable at 25-35 years, when they average 40 m tall and 50 cm diameter at breast height. Our radiata forests today are extensive enough (some 700,000 hectares) to provide all the timber we need for housing and domestic use in the foreseeable future, and a growing surplus for export. The heartwood is light in colour and light to handle, ideal for building the modern frame houses favoured in New Zealand. (They are resistant to earthquake shock.) It is calculated that the average-sized house requires about 14 cubic metres of timber, which is the equivalent to 30 cubic metres of wood in the log, or approximately one truckload of logs loaded in the forest. To eliminate attacks of fungi and insect pests during the first decade or two of use in building, such timber is 'tanalised', that is, treated with a lethal form of chemical tanning under pressure which drives the fungicide-insecticide into the sawn wood.

Typical of many introduced species, radiata, in the drier areas of our country, has become vigorous enough to 'go native'. It will regenerate freely from its own seed fallen amid the decaying debris after each clear felling. Birds, wind and other agents - especially man - distribute the ripe seeds adventitiously elsewhere, creating problems of management to eliminate the

A typical grouping of toadstools and layered fungi studied in a eucalypt forest where the light encouraged a gorse bush to grow. Opossums, incidentally, are fond of browsing the tender young flowers of gorse.

63

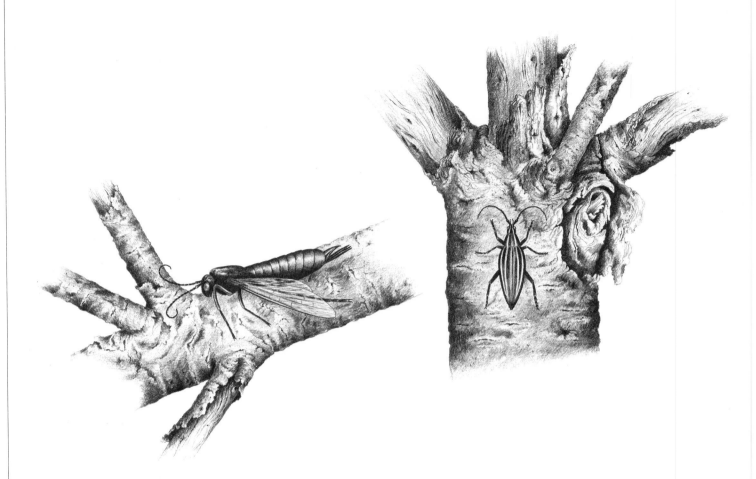

Man proposes, Nature disposes. In any Man-devised monoculture for his material benefit - fields of grain or forests of one species - Nature endeavours to restore the balance which obtains in the wild, where parasites and predators ensure that no one species alone shall overwhelm the ecology to the exclusion of others sharing the habitat.

The larvae of wood and bark-boring moths and beetles are swift to colonise large commercial radiata stands. They enter by way of a natural wound, such as a wind-broken branch, or a careless axe-blaze marking a forest path. Some borer grubs tunnel deep into the heartwood, feeding there for a year or two before pupating. Once such an entry is effected, a host of other parasites follows: the larvae of ghost and other moths, weevils and beetles, as well as moulds and fungi which soften and render the tough wood digestible with the protein and bacteria they produce by the thread-like mycelium process.

The striped long-horn beetle of our native forests, *Navomorphla sulcata*, (right) freely attacks radiata, boring holes in which to deposit its eggs.

The large and vivid horntail wasp, *Sirex noctilio* (the female is steel-blue, the male has a golden-yellow abdomen), accidentally introduced from Europe, probably in pinewood packing cases, has become a widespread pest (left). The female drills her long ovipositor deep into the living wood to deposit her egg and - another seeming miracle of evolution - the egg itself is already equipped with the spores of the fungus which will assist the hatching larva to digest its diet of timber. Swarms of adult horntail wasps emerge in early autumn from their burrows in the now unthrifty radiata trees and ascend above the forest to mate in the air.

Biological warfare has been the forester's answer, i.e. the introduction of the horntail wasp's natural predators, in

particular the remarkable ichneumon wasp or fly, *Rhyssa persuosoria*. Having located, by some means unknown to us, the precise spot where a horntail grub is hidden in its burrow, the female *Rhyssa* elevates her tail to unsheath her long ovipositor, then proceeds to drill through the bark and wood with astonishing accuracy to reach and deposit her egg beside a horntail larva. This she 'stings' with the same instrument, injecting a sedative which immobilises it. The *Rhyssa* egg soon hatches and the parasitic grub feeds at first on the non-vital parts of the living, paralysed horntail grub!

Attracted to the new hole excavated by the horntail borer by the resin oozing from the puncture, a smaller winged parasite, the ebony-coloured *Ibalia leucospoides*, having only a frail, hair-like ovipositor, takes a short cut, simply inserting this probe down the ready-made shaft until it reaches a horntail egg or young grub.

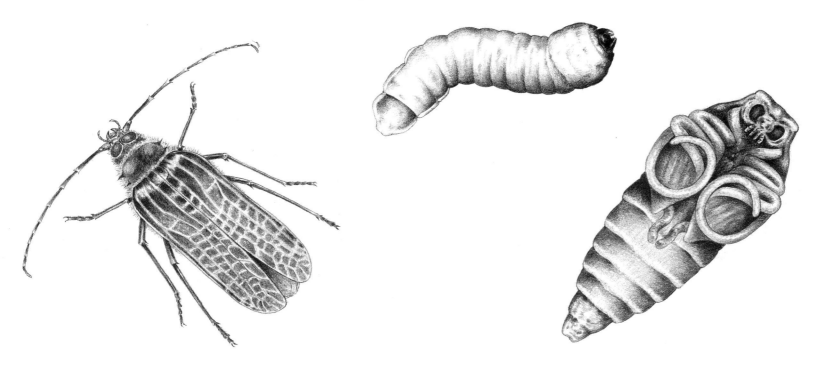

vigorous pines when these appear where they are not desirable, as in nature reserves and forests maintained for endemic species. Male and female radiata cones grow on the same tree: winged pollen grains are wafted by the wind to fertilise the ripened mother cell as each scale of the female cone opens to admit the male spore. However, commercial foresters find that too many 'weeds' of unwanted plants compete for the open space left by clear-felling. They prefer to replant seedling radiata, eucalypt and other exotics in orderly rows, each block of the forest filled with young plants of uniform age and height, raised in tree nurseries. This facilitates after-care and access for weeding and pruning. For this purpose, it is routine in well-managed exotic forests, after each clear-felling, to burn the top and lop by controlled firing, and/or by bulldozing the 'trash' into heaps for burning in a dry spell. This operation means death to most wildlife at ground level which has survived the felling and extraction phase.

Fire is both a weapon and the most dreaded danger for the forester. Mismanaged burn-offs, a picnic fire, an unextinguished cigarette, are responsible for the frequent fires which destroy large areas of exotic forest annually. The debris of dead branches and needles shed in maturing radiata, and the naturally moulted bark in tall eucalypt forests are highly inflammable.

To the naturalist the exotic forest becomes attractive during its first few years of growth, when the young trees (some 1500 radiata seedlings to each hectare) are one to two metres tall, their sturdy green fronds reaching to the light above a miscellaneous groundcover of wild grasses, flowers, and young shrubs - mostly introduced 'weed' species. Such plantations are often fenced and may be rarely visited by the forester. They rapidly become sanctuaries for a fascinating fauna of invading mammals, birds, insects and other animals, and a splendid living herbarium for the curious botanist.

The well-known native huhu beetle grub, up to 8 cm in length, once regarded as a tasty delicacy by the Maori, is the larva of the longhorn beetle *Prionoplus reticularis*, which flies buzzingly by night. The female lays her eggs in clusters in holes and insect burrows in dead or dying trees, and not infrequently in rotten (untanalised) timber of old buildings. Maori eel-fishermen tell us that they still bait their overnight flax or nylon lines with living huhu grubs obtained by breaking open rotten logs.

OVER PAGE: The exotic forest

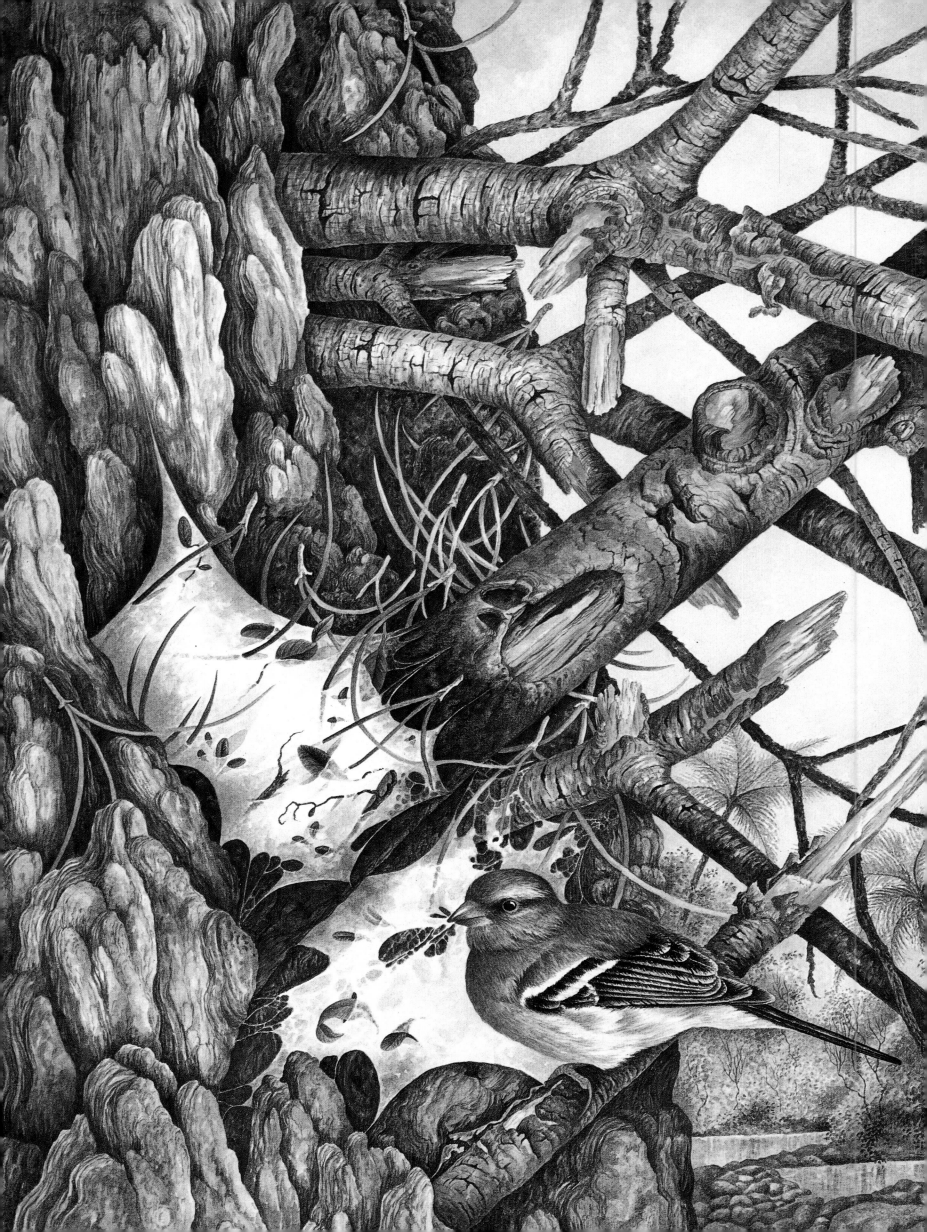

The grey warbler is at home in low cover of both native and exotic forest.

Exotic finches may be numerous, flocking to feed on the seeds of the fast-growing annual and perennial plants which have colonised the bare ground, their species dependent on the nature of the soil; certain plants flourish in calcareous ground, others prefer clay or sand. Goldfinch, greenfinch, redpoll and yellowhammer are early arrivals to feed and breed while the trees are no more than breast high. Chaffinches prefer taller trees to nest in, but throng to young plantations during the late summer and autumn seed harvest of the 'weeds'.

Grey warbler, fantail, silver-eye and dunnock, all birds which like plenty of sunlight, roam the young plantations in

search of their insect food: larvae and adults of moths, butterflies, flies, grasshoppers, spiders, stick insects, praying mantis, aphids, etc. Thrush and blackbird are there, tackling slugs, snails, worms, and the annual crop of fleshy berries such as blackberry, boxwood, wineberry, and wild strawberry. Kingfishers hunt lizards and mice, and snatch up the unwary small bird. Wild deer, normally resident in native forest, invade the growing exotic plantation, where they find rich browsing by night upon the mixture of young trees and rampant ground-cover. By day they are well hidden where they lie down to sleep or chew the cud at rest.

A sambar stag; this deer is spread sparsely in young pine forests.

Year by year the planted trees grow taller. At ten years of age radiata has formed a shady canopy averaging 15 m high. The groundcover changes. Only shade-tolerant plants and animals survive upon the thickening carpet of pine needles and shed lower branches which have died off for lack of sunlight. Depending on what the forester intends as the end product of each parcel of radiata forest, he will thin and prune the trees; from the original maximum of 1500 at planting to as few as 200 per hectare at clear-felling, which takes place at twenty-five years when the average height is 46 m.

Board-grade timber must be as free as possible from knots caused by unpruned side-branches, as it is used in building where it can be seen. Careful pruning with the long-handled shears opens up the forest for walking, by man and beast, as well as providing more light for the survival of some of the original ground fauna and flora.

It is less important to prune trees grown for framing timber (knots are hidden in building), or for pulping. Pruning, which must be done by hand, is expensive, and often today the less accessible plantations are not pruned, or even thinned. Long before they mature these forests become impenetrable for walking, choked with stunted and dead trees denied the sunlight by the more dominant faster-growing individual trees. A forester in Scotland declared to us that planted pine forests, allowed to grow untended, eventually produced fewer timber trees, but these dominants yielded the tallest and best quality wood for building purposes. (We were there looking for the smaller deer - roe and sika - which find secure daytime cover in the dense understorey of weak and dying pines under the dominant crowns of the taller trees. From this cover the deer emerge at dusk to browse younger plantations and farm and heath land, as sika, sambar and red deer do in New Zealand.)

In the middle years of the well-pruned forest, there is still much to observe as we stroll under the darkened canopy upon a silent carpet of pine needles. In summer we may surprise a deer, a wild pig or smaller mammal asleep in the forest coolness. We may notice the droppings of other animals - rats and opossums, even occasionally a hedgehog - but what are they feeding on? The groundcover looks bare, with a few ferns, scattered pine cones, and groups of fungi (chiefly toadstools) in damper spots.

OPPOSITE: Chaffinches are at home in mature forests, especially of pines. The female is responsible for building the exquisitely fashioned nest cup, a foundation of fine rootlets bound with green moss, grey lichen and spider silk. She lines it with feathers just before she lays her four or five eggs which are attractively spotted and scribbled with roseate markings (above).

BELOW: Two common toadstools of a pine forest, *Boletus rhacodes* (left) and *Macrolepiota rachodes*.

71

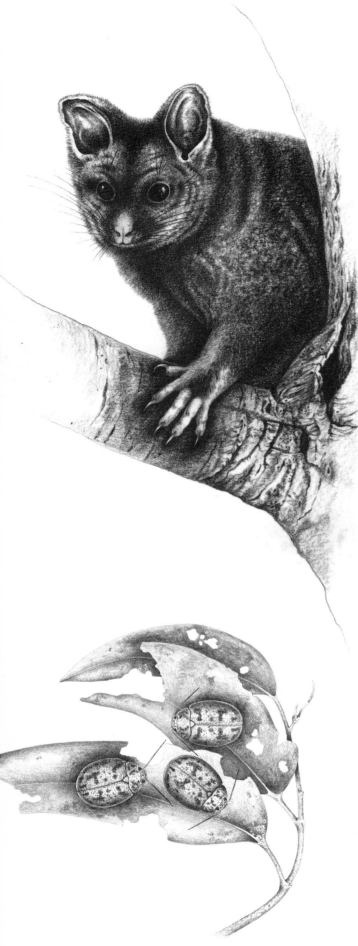

Eucalypt beetle *Paropsis charybdis*

One would expect the rats in an exotic forest to be the non-climbing *Rattus norvegicus*, twice the size and weight of the ship rat, *R. rattus*, but recent trapping tests have established that the rat of both New Zealand's exotic and native forests is the latter, sometimes called the black rat. It has a long, partly prehensile tail, and climbs up the trunk and amid the foliage almost with the agility of a squirrel. A few years ago scientist M.N. Clout, using apple-baited traps to catch opossums in 15-year-old (second crop) radiata forest, found the bait largely devoured by ship rats clever enough to enter these live traps without triggering the treadle door. Using break-back rat traps baited with cheese resulted in the death of 22 rats over three nights. An examination of their stomach contents proved that they had been feeding principally on the larvae of forest moths (it was late July - midwinter), flies (maggot and pupae), and, another surprise, cave wetas. Unlike the common weta, which is heavily protected by sharp spines, cave wetas are soft-bodied insects with extremely long legs and antennae. They find the cool darkness of forests to their liking. Hiding by day in holes and under rotting bark, they browse by night on vegetation, but may scavenge the remains of small dead insects. Evidently the nocturnal ship rat finds wetas highly edible, and accessible. The rat was also shown to feed on beetles and spiders, but plant material eaten was limited to a little moss, fungi and pine needles.

It was no surprise that pine seed did not appear in this sample of the ship rat's diet in a radiata forest. In nature *P. radiata* seeds can remain viable for several years, enclosed tightly in the cone, which opens only under hot, dry conditions, usually at midsummer, or after a forest fire. Opossums, which have an enormously varied vegetarian diet, but prefer the tender growth of buds and new leaves, freely browse those of radiata. Interestingly, in an analysis of the stomach contents of 550 opossums killed on farmland near Waverley (July-September) it was found that conifer pollen, from both radiata and macrocarpa, was a main food present in some. In trials with caged opossums, the animals licked at pollen from male flowers, and also inhaled the pollen through the open mouth.

Eucalypt plantations at all times allow more light to filter from the sky through their sparser branches and linear leaves, so that the forest floor supports a variety of shrubby plants, ferns and fungi. Although the ground is generally drier, there is a moist humus protected by the constantly shed bark of the gum trees.

Eucalyptus trees attract numerous parasites. One such is the tortoise beetle *Paropsis charybdis*, shaped like a tortoise and varying in colour from brown through yellow to crimson. Its defence mechanism when disturbed is to erect two tubes at its rear and eject a liquid smelling vilely of eucalyptus, and drop to the ground. Normally it hibernates under loose bark. It lays rows of eggs on the surface of the leaves, which both adult and larva greedily devour. Another feeder on eucalypt leaves - perhaps a more welcome visitor because of its beauty - is the gum emperor moth (see over).

Tiny riflemen on a eucalyptus tree

The beautiful gum emperor moth, *Antheraea eucalypti,* with the largest wingspan of all our moths - 14 cm - was deliberately introduced from Australia for its handsome appearance both as caterpillar and as winged moth. It is now common in the warmer districts wherever eucalyptus trees have been planted in number as forest or orchard shelter belts, and even in city streets. Its caterpillars are bizarrely beautiful, a vivid green with paler stripes, each segment furnished with blue-tipped tufts of yellow spines.

After feeding on gum leaves all summer, the caterpillar is some 9 cm in length when it spins its curious cocoon of layers of silk, and its larval length shrinks to become a pupa. The silk layers harden into a thick, waterproof shell as tough as that of a hazelnut, and much the same size. Look for these dark cocoons attached to a gum or pepper tree twig. It is worth bringing the twig with its cocoon indoors to study the emergence of the moth which normally takes place early in the evening of a warm spring day.

First there is a scraping sound as the new-born moth cuts a circular door with a sharp spine developed for that sole purpose at the base of each undeveloped upper wing, as it turns around in its prison. At the same time it softens the silk with a solvent fluid. Presently the moth squeezes forth, to hang like ragged brown velvet curtains for about an hour, its huge wings expanding to their full beauty as air and blood are pumped into the veins, revealing the characteristic black-ringed eye spots. If a female moth emerges - she is stouter and has a larger cocoon than the male - she is sluggish and disinclined to fly. She awaits the arrival of a male, who tracks her down by the pheromes of her scent wafted far on the night air. The adult moth has a brief lifespan; once mating is completed, the male dies and so does the female as soon as she has deposited her neat row of yellow eggs on the leaves of the food tree. The adults do not feed; their mouthparts are degenerate. Body fat stored during the caterpillar stage suffices to cover the nuptial period.

Commercial strains of fast-growing poplar are often planted as fire-breaks in damp areas, and to utilise wet ground where pines and gum trees will not thrive. Their pale, trembling leaves break the monotony of the vast monocultured evergreen exotic forest areas; in the autumn the poplar groves are a golden glow, relieving the dark landscape before the leaves are shed and winter boughs are bare 'where late the wild birds sang'. Traditionally the smooth white wood of mature poplar, cut to veneer thinness, was used for making boxes and containers for cheese and other food products.

Kaingaroa Forest, east of Lake Taupo, is said to be the largest area under radiata pine in the world, planted and managed by Man. Happily much of the area is open to the public, accessible by good motor roads, selected walking tracks and camping sites. More to the point, to delight the naturalist's eye some stands of mature trees have been left to grow beyond the normal felling age, in effect re-creating the attractive habitat of natural Monterey pine forest found in California, and also illustrating botanist Cockayne's well-known principle that 'the warfare between the primitive New Zealand inhabitants and their alien invaders is waged almost entirely under conditions where Man takes a hand'. Left alone, New Zealand soil would gradually revert to original endemic forest. In these few Kaingaroa mature reserves, the process has already begun.

With more light penetrating from the sparser, taller treetops, the natural understorey of shade-tolerant native plants is already established. It is remarkably beautiful for walking in, or merely seen from your car. As if by magic the columnar tree ferns have lifted their graceful crowns of lacework fronds from the rich humus layer of dead and disintegrated pine debris. Strolling there, we perceive the soft blanket of tiny ferns, native orchids and mosses, aerially arrived as spores during the last decade. Fantails with their frilly, flirting tails seem most at home, but in patient watching we have seen both rifleman (opposite) and tomtit happily fly-hunting around the stout pine-boles and young ponga poles. The grey warbler sings freely. The chaffinches have long been in residence.

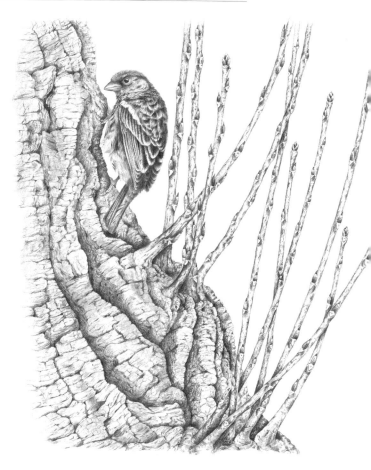

Sparrow on poplar.

Heodictyon cibarius, the basket fungus, drawn from a specimen found on a hillside clearing in a pine plantation.

Riches of the Wetland

In these savage, liquid plains,
Only known to wandering swains,
Where the mossy riv'let strays,
Far from human haunts and ways,
All on Nature you depend,
And life's poor season peaceful spend.
                Robert Burns (1759-96)

The shallow wetland, in its transition from lake and swamp to vegetated marsh and finally to forest, is one of the richest wildlife ecosystems in the natural world, supporting a food chain consisting of innumerable species of plants and animals. It is a delight to study the diverse and ever-changing worlds of reedy ponds, small lakes, peat fens or bogs, as well as larger areas of fresh water under the open sky.

It is exciting to watch the diurnal birds typical of this habitat: the pukekos, herons and stilts prefer shallow water through which they walk and stalk on their long legs; grey, shoveler and mallard ducks can be seen feeding on the surface; above the water the welcome swallows will be taking insects on the wing. A watchful harrier may be floating on graceful broad pinions as it searches the swamp vegetation for frogs, rodents and unwary birds.

Much of the wildlife is hidden, heard but seldom seen. Among the shy birds are the skulking bittern, the crake, rail and fernbird: beneath the surface live numerous fish species as well as countless aquatic insects and their larvae - every cubic centimetre contains microscopic life. The luxuriant waterside flora - sedges, reeds, raupo - and the encroaching forest trees which like wet feet, provide cover for singing birds, croaking frogs and silent lizards. Here yet more insects abound, crawling, flying, buzzing and stridulating.

The wetland, where Man seldom treads, is a natural sanctuary for wildlife. To the thoughtful naturalist it is a microcosm of the birth and cycle of life on earth. The splendid moving clouds in the sky above are formed of purified vapour drawn up by the heat of the sun from all water surfaces - sea, lake, river, swamp, and the morning dew - to fall as clean rain, renewing the life-giving moisture by which we live.

It was in the warmth of the new-born oceans under the sun that, about 3000 million years ago, the first stirrings of life appeared- the unicellular algae and bacteria. Today we observe the same cycle of life in every body of natural fresh water, be it lake, pond, marsh, lily pool or even the open rain-butt under the

Circus approximans, known as the swamp harrier, looks and behaves like a small eagle, but feeds mostly on carrion, including animals killed on the road.

OPPOSITE: Unique to New Zealand is the shy, mouse-like fernbird, *Bowdleria punctata*, which inhabits the thick vegetation to be found in swamps. The nest is built low down, often over water - even salt water where high tides invade an estuary. Seldom seen, the male bird can be called into view if he hears an imitation of its clicking call. He is strongly territorial, guarding his quarter-hectare feeding and breeding property from rival males.

PRECEDING PAGES: Riches of the wetland: a typical swampland scene.

Although born as free-swimming upright fish, flounders soon take to lying flat on the bottom, where their upper surface matches in colour the mud or sand around them. The eye on the lower side, now useless, migrates to join the one on the upper side. Another remarkable fact is that three New Zealand species have both eyes on the left-hand side of the head; they live in deeper water than the other 'right-eye' flounders. Of the latter, the yellow-belly flounder *Rhombosolea leporina* (up to 50cm in length, below) is one of the most abundant, swimming in estuaries and following the tide far upriver. It is a very tasty fish - the patiki-totara beloved of Maori and Pakeha alike. The smaller black or mud flounder *R. retiaria* travels even farther upstream, and is sometimes quite abundant in freshwater lakes or swamps with outlets to the sea.

eaves. Green algae first appear: their pigment (chlorophyll) absorbs energy from sunlight by the process known as photosynthesis: the manufacture of life-supporting food (sugars, carbohydrates) in combination with the elements of air and water (hydrogen and oxygen). Probably the first algae multiplied by simple division; later they developed spores which floated in water and air, as they do today.

About 1000 million years ago the first animals - the minute protozoas or protista - were born as free-swimming browsers of the algae and bacteria. More complex forms followed, some remaining vegetarian, others becoming carnivorous, many both. The extraordinary hydra we see in fresh water today attached themselves to solid objects and developed fine tentacles (*cilia*) like the sea anenomes, to collect free-swimming plankton. So named after the many-headed monster of Greek mythology, hydra today possess sting cells to paralyse their victim. They propagate by laying free-floating eggs, or budding off a limb, which feeds at first umbilically through the tubes of the adult digestive system. After growing its own scavenging tentacles, it seals the parental connection and moves off, eventually to attach itself to a new foundation.

The first backboned fish swam in prehistoric seas about 400 million years ago, later than the primitive marine worms, sponges and jellyfish. From the salty ocean, moved by tides created by the pull of moon and sun, the prolific free-swimming plankton with its developing chain of larger predators drifted into the estuaries of the rivers of primeval continents. Early waterside vegetation already existed - the as yet flowerless ferns, horsetails, liverworts and mosses, reproducing by spores.

Adapting to fresh water, they gradually penetrated far upstream, entering lakes and swamps, diversifying to produce new species in geographical isolation. Some, like the ancestors of our native trout *Galaxias* (whitebait) and introduced salmon, returned seasonally to the sea, obeying an irresistible impulse of inherited memory. Today some whitebait species return only to spawn at the sea's edge, but the salmon does the opposite, feeding in the ocean until adult and ascending to spawn in the headwaters of rivers. Yet when trapped by blocked outlets in lakes and swamps, salmon, galaxias and several marine fishes survived to breed as new purely freshwater forms.

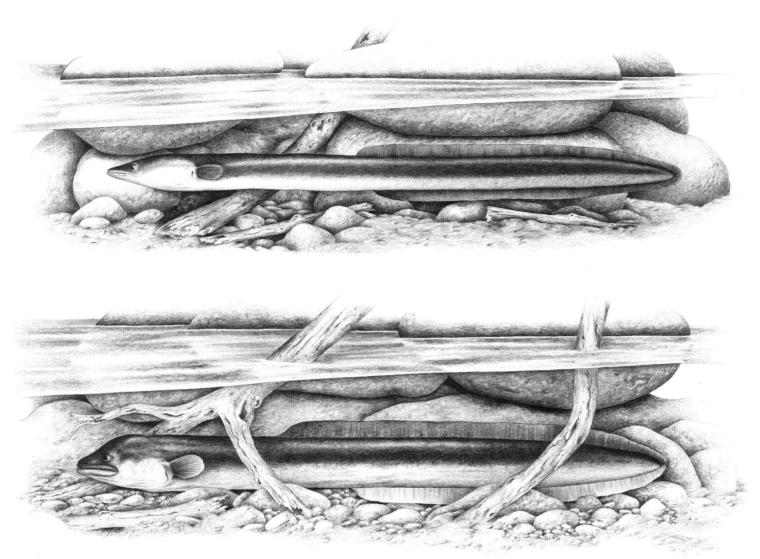

New Zealand boasts the largest freshwater eels in the world, up to 2 metres long and weighing up to 50 kilograms. The full-grown adults provide a valuable fishery as they leave swamps and rivers and are trapped on their way to the sea. Somewhere - still unknown but presumed to be in the Coral Sea - they gather in warm deep tropic waters to spawn and die. The tiny, leaf-like larvae rise to the surface and, feeding on plankton as they drift with the current, take about two years to return to New Zealand. Millions of these tiny elvers - about 60 mm long, semi-transparent and known as 'glass eels' - swim up every river, becoming an important link in the freshwater food chain. They wriggle successfully up sheer wet rock surfaces and reservoir dams, and follow by night the merest trickle of water to reach small ponds and every sort of wetland habitat, even garden lily pools. Preying on insects, water-snails and aquatic larvae, males take between ten and twenty years to mature; the larger females take longer.

At last the night arrives when the adult ceases to feed and sets forth to retrace its mysterious dramatic voyage. In preparation for this 3200-kilometre swim into deep ocean, its fins and eyes enlarge, the mouth and alimentary system shrink, and the reproductive organs swell with ripening eggs or sperm.

The New Zealand long-finned eel, *Anguilla dieffenbachii,* largest of the world's freshwater species, travels far inland to reach mountain streams and lakes. The smaller, short-finned *A. australis,* distinguished also by its shorter dorsal (back) fin and small pointed head, inhabits New Zealand, Australia, Tasmania, Norfolk Island and other sub-tropical islands to the north. It does not travel so far up-river, preferring fresh water nearer to sea, but like the New Zealand long-finned, this species migrates to the Coral Sea to spawn and to die.

The white-faced heron, *Ardea novaehollandiae*, rarely recorded in New Zealand before 1940, is now the most numerous and obvious of the heron family, haunting fresh and salt water alike, visiting tidal lagoons, rivers, lakes, swamps, farm dams and even garden pools. Here it stalks shallow water fish, frogs, large insects and small life of many species. Sometimes it stands perfectly still, ready to strike what may swim near - perhaps a rat or an unwary duckling. At other moments it moves slowly forward, raising a foot to stir the surface of the water and surprise aquatic life into betraying movement.

Captures are swallowed whole; large items may be carried ashore and battered on the ground to subdue their struggles. It is surprising to watch this heron gulping down a large flounder, still alive. It is turned around in the long bill so that it is swallowed head first; for a while its progress down the long elastic neck is visible as an uncomfortable bulge!

If a large eel is extracted from its hole in the bank of a river or swamp, its slimy, twisting, tenacious resistance to being swallowed, even after being battered, may result in the heron regurgitating it several times before it is subdued enough to remain in the bird's crop.

After a fish feed, the heron meticulously preens the slime from its plumage. As it has no oil gland at the base of the tail for this purpose (as the majority of birds have), it 'dry-cleans' its feathers with a special talc or powder consisting of the brittle scale of the disintegrating feathers of the breast and body, applied with the tip of the bill and by rubbing the back of the head against this powder source. In addition, the longest toe has a serrated edge for combing the head and neck, which are inaccessible to the beak.

Fine feathers make this regal bird even more handsome by mid-winter when long silky plumes are assumed for the nuptial dance early in July. This takes place at the nesting site, often out of

human view at the top of a tall conifer. The male brings offerings of sticks to his lady and indulges in a clumsy-looking display of waving wings as he prances on long legs.

As soon as the three to five blue-green eggs are laid, the pair share incubation, rearing and feeding duties with equal zeal. At about six weeks the young herons, well-grown on the fish and other delicacies regurgitated by their parents, are ready to make their own way into their competitive ecosystem of marsh and estuary, fortunately at this moment of early summer well supplied with newly-hatched aquatic fry, water snails and swimming larvae.

Not all fledglings survive. When trying out their wings in a summer gale, the tree-top born herons are not infrequently blown away before they can sustain normal flight to escape prowling cat or stoat.

The swamp is most accessible to us in summer drought. Where the water level falls and naked ground becomes exposed it is swiftly colonised by a host of plants whose seeds were stranded amid swathes of dying algae and duckweed. For a while we can walk with dry feet to study this Lilliputian jungle of flowering sedges, rushes, buttercups, pondweed and willow herb species, along with sundry vigorous low-growing grasses, clovers, trefoil and scarlet pimpernel.

This colourful margin is a loafing ground for families of ducks, stilts and pukekos, resting, preening or dabbling in the plant cover for the abundant insect, slug and snail life. At night other animals come to feed and drink - hedgehog, rat, stoat, weasel, ferret and wild pig.

Pukeko parties enjoy family outings; the well-feathered children of the spring brood will even help the downy black chicks of the later hatch to find food. They soon learn to copy the adult habit of plucking a juicy grass or sedge stem and holding it up in the toes of one foot, parrot-fashion, to nibble it piecemeal. They will eagerly seize your picnic bread and eat in this dainty fashion.

The huge scarlet bill and forehead of *Porphyrio melanotus*, the pukeko or swamp hen, has significance for easy recognition by its kind as it stalks through thick damp vegetation. Even if not seen in taller cover, its frequent call - an ear-piercing scream - serves as an additional recognition signal.

Evidently the black stilt, descended from the stilts of Australia, settled in New Zealand in pre-Maori times, when the land was covered with virgin mature forest, and only the mountains were treeless. Isolated in this cool upland habitat, it became larger and darker, and in due course vulnerable to the swathe of ground predators introduced by Man. But the somewhat smaller, elegant pied stilt, *Himantopus leucocephalus*, (left) was a much later arrival, self-introduced from Australia and not yet common in New Zealand when the white settler arrived. As a lover of open country, this remarkably tame wader spread rapidly throughout the islands wherever there were swamps, ponds and reservoirs. Today it even nests beside municipal lakes and sewage farms.

After the breeding season the pied stilt forms large flocks which feed along the tidal shore. At high tide when fully fed it rests in colourful regiments, frequently half asleep on one crimson leg.

Both the Maori and Pakeha settlers were at first happy that Captain Cook and other explorers, whalers and sailors released domestic pigs into the wild so that they would become a source of much-needed protein in a land completely lacking endemic ground mammals. Today, those of us who are not keen hunters regret the introductions, for this large, omnivorous beast throve not only on the roots and vegetarian foods of the forests but also sought out with its strong questing snout and keen sense of smell all it could sink its powerful teeth into - especially the hapless flightless birds nesting in burrows, the endemic large snails, the lizards, and other small life uprooted from earth and ground cover.

Late last century the wild pig became so numerous that it started harassing sheep and taking new-born lambs. It is much scarcer today, due to both hunting and farming practices which destroy its natural habitat, damp, swampy forests.

Although derived from the large, plump, thin-haired domestic breeds, wild swine in New Zealand have tended to revert towards the ancestral wild boar, *Sus scrofa*, in appearance; they are longer in the leg, with ridges of long back hair, hence the name razorbacks.

During the day they lie up in couches made with the snout in thick vegetation or in a favourite mud wallow. The sow, with perhaps two of her latest litters (up to a dozen born in each) around her, is sociable, whereas the adult boar remains somewhat aloof, always ready to attack a rival male approaching a sow in heat. The lower pair of canine teeth have developed into scimitar tusks projecting from the jaw. Hunters tell tall stories about the savage attacks of a wild boar at bay, but in fact the tusks are secondary sexual characteristics, like the spurs on a male chicken, useful to impress and intimidate rather than be employed in wasteful fighting.

Year by year aquatic vegetation dies back during the winter, and the shallow swamp adds another layer of detritus to the bottom. A hidden world of scavenging creatures inhabits this lowly stratum: worms eat rotten vegetation, leeches and flukes parasitise snails, frogs and larval insects - even fish and swimming birds. In the spring the water temperature rises and insect eggs and larvae develop rapidly into the imago or perfect adult stage. Myriads of these insects take wing as they leave the water - flies, gnats, mosquitoes and beetles predominate, and the largest are the gaudy dragonflies.

They are all ready to mate, and the honeymoon is almost non-existent. Mayflies live only a few hours, and have no mouths through which they can pass food. Dancing in the air with his mate, the male dies as soon as he has inseminated the female, who descends to the surface of the water to deposit the egg clusters from her abdomen. The eggs sink to the bottom, to develop later as larval grubs.

The nursery-web spider, *Dolomedes minor*, weaves her cage of white silk around the top twigs of tall swamp and bush vegetation as a protection for her eggs and tiny spiderlings, which she guards until the day the latter take off to explore the world on their silken parachutes.

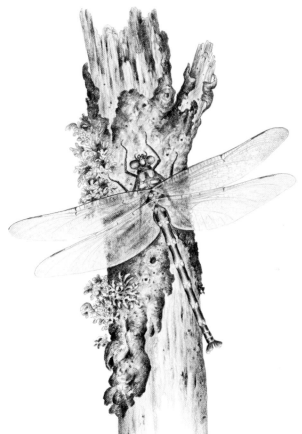

The dragonflies and damselflies which appear above every swamp at midsummer develop from carnivorous larvae living for one or more years under water. The adult flies survive several days of feeding upon insects seized on the wing or at rest. Energised by the hot sun, the male dragonfly pursues the female, suddenly grasping her neck with special claspers at the end of his abdomen or tail. He holds her firmly thus during mating, a method which is unique among insects. Before approaching the female, the male transfers sperm from his genital opening (close to the claspers) to a special pouch (vesicle) on the underside of the front portion of his abdomen. Carried thus in tandem flight, the female curls her tail forwards and upwards to bring her genital opening against the vesicle pouch of the male to effect fertilisation.

Kowhai, *Sophora tetraptera*, loveliest of the native flowering trees, thrives well where its roots can reach damp ground.

As water-tolerant trees invade the vegetated swamp, it becomes a marsh, with little open water save during winter rains. Cabbage trees (*Cordyline australis*), nikau palm (*Rhopalostylis sapida)*, manuka and the taller kanuka (*Leptospermum*) are some of the earliest trespassers on the drying wetland. The splendid kahikatea or white pine (*Podocarpus dacrydiodes)* eventually dominates, rising to 40 metres tall; these were the giant forest trees of the swampy Hauraki Plain so much admired by Captain Cook in 1769 when he was rowed up the river he named Thames.

Kahikatea, *Podocarpus dacry-diodes,* showing mature tree, young trees, ripe seeds atop their fleshy receptacles, and male cones. Tui, bellbird and native pigeon eat the ripe fruit.

River Life

I will walk in the meadows by some gliding stream, and there contemplate the Lillies that take no care, and those other various little living creatures that are not only created but fed (man knows not how) by the goodness of the God of Nature . . . This is my purpose - to be quiet and go angling.

Izaak Walton (1593-1683)

Later writers captured that same mood of contemplation and freedom from care which the river induces in those who love to stroll by the swift bright water, laden with its burden of dissolved particles of earth and rock, its animal and plant life. 'The river glideth at his own sweet will' - thus simply did William Wordsworth express its enduring strength and independence; and Elizabeth Barrett Browning its eternal mystery: 'what was he doing, the great God Pan, down in the reeds by the river?'

Our first pleasure in New Zealand rivers was in exploring the Maraetotara and Tukituki which flow north from the Silver Hills into Hawke Bay. On that hot summer day we were surrounded by nostalgic reminders of the flora and fauna of home streams of Britain. Yellowhammers stammered from golden gorse. Charms of goldfinches more numerous than any ever seen in England tinkled their happy songs as they fed on thistle seeds parachuting in the warm air. New-fledged sparrrow, starling and greenfinch parties chirped and trilled in nearby paddock and bush, a little apart, as it were, from native birds. Piwakawaka (fantail) warblers snatched up flies disturbed by our feet, their long silvery tails flickering from side to side. Picturesquely atop a tall weeping willow a young kingfisher, azure-winged and tailed, squawked hungrily, awaiting a fish handout from parents perched watchfully on boughs overhanging the deep pool below.

Sea-run trout darted around our shoulders when we cooled off in this pool, trying to identify at eye level the small life of aquatic insects and plants, most of them common to Britain too. Species of mimulus, water buttercup, white starwort, water poppy, floating pondweed (*Potamogeton*), true water cress and the green tresses of hairweed or milfoil (*Myriophyllum*). Dragonflies and the abundant blue and purple little damselflies vied with Australian welcome swallows (which look so like English swallows) in flashing pursuit of aerial insects rising reborn from their long nymph life under the water.

OPPOSITE: The banded rail likes to skulk and feed in low wet vegetation, nesting in drier cover on the nearest bank.

Above the river a string of feral goats, alleged by the farmer to be useful in cleaning up noxious weeds, gambolled agilely upon a steep bluff, contentedly nibbling, as goats will, a little of each - young gorse, yarrow, fennel, thistle, tree fern, five-finger, manuka, mahoe, narcotic foxglove, poisonous tutu and hemlock. Tutu leaves and berries are fatal to all farm animals if eaten on an empty stomach, yet here were dainty silver-eye warblers eagerly pecking at the juicy new seeds of tutu hanging in graceful racemes from long fluted branches. (Maori women knew how to separate this tasty juice from the lethal seeds by straining through a flaxen sieve.)

Along these southern Hawke's Bay rivers, a new Australian bird had lately colonised. The small, strikingly handsome, black-fronted dotterel, *Charadrius melanops*, pied and tawny of plumage, with black collar above white breast, and scarlet bill and legs, was first noticed in 1954. Today it nests sparsely on most North Island and some South Island riverbanks. Interestingly, we found it shares this habitat with the larger, more numerous and widespread native banded dotterel, *C. bicinctus*, but the two coexist without undue competition, the smaller dotterel feeding almost exclusively along the water's edge and scraping a shallow nest for its three mottled eggs close above the flood-line. The banded dotterel is quite catholic in feeding on insects and small molluscs - it even chased after the plentiful white butterflies in the river valley - well above the jetsam line and in nearby paddocks, dunes and ploughed ground. It nests in such places along rivers throughout New Zealand up to and beyond the tree-line, as far south as Stewart and Auckland Islands.

The banded dotterel is the most numerous of the three *Charadrius* waders breeding in New Zealand. Somewhat drab and inconspicuous in winter plumage it puts on a black collar and a rich chestnut breast band during the nesting season.

90

Strangely, although the black-fronted dotterel self-introduced itself from Australia, there is no evidence that it is other than a sedentary resident in New Zealand, whereas a large proportion of banded dotterels migrate across the Tasman (an unusual latitudinal movement, but also undertaken by juvenile gannets) to spend the winter in southern Australia. They seem to be mostly young dotterels, and may spend a whole year abroad, yet have never been recorded as breeding in Australia.

North Island rivers enjoy a warmer climate than those of the South Island (too warm for the nesting of certain littoral birds which come north only after they have finished breeding beside South Island rivers - as we shall presently describe), but the air was chill enough on the day we began our trek along New Zealand's longest river, 450 km from source to sea. The infant Waikato issues as a snow-fed series of rivulets under the barren rocks of the still-active volcanic peak of Ruapehu, highest North Island mountain. Little waterfalls drip from mini-glaciers and bicker across treeless sands to build up a substantial torrent, known as the Tongariro River, as it spurts by white cascades through ravines and the first hardy trees. There are still mountain blue duck here, feeding on caddis and other flies and their larvae, but becoming rarer because of human trampers, canoeists and white-water rafting - to the annoyance of peaceful Izaak Waltons plying their trout rods in the broader lower reaches of this Tongariro water, before it sallies forth into Lake Taupo near Turangi.

We visit Taupo in another chapter; here let us rejoin the Waikato where it issues from that lake and foams over the

The handsome black-fronted dotterel, a welcome addition to New Zealand's shingle rivers, arrived from Australia first colonising the Hawke's Bay area. Today it is spreading southwards and has begun to nest in the South Island.

91

spectacular Huka Falls. Maori legends tell of the drowning of their early explorers daring to shoot these falls in their canoes. The Huka Falls have blocked the access to Lake Taupo of coarse, 'unsporting' fish such as grass and koi carp and catfish introduced in the Waikato farther downriver. Millions of elvers, born perhaps 2000 km away in the Coral Sea, have also been blocked after wriggling around the down-stream hydro-electric dams in side trickles of water through the bankside vegetation, to populate the local lakes and rivers. We have watched this migration where the black mass of young two-year-old eels congregates below the sheer concrete walls of the hydro-electric dams of some eight power stations between Taupo and the sea. Large trout, which cannot surmount the dam, were there, feeding on the elvers as some fell from the wet surface, up which hundreds more were squirming.

The Waikato below Taupo becomes more and more sophisticated, tamed and groomed to man's needs. There are still minor waterfalls and chasms of quiet water rich in wild birds and flowers, but the deepest gorges have been dammed, raising the water level to create long narrow lakes, controlled by sluice and headrace. Artificial Lake Karapiro with its 42 m high dam, is 24 kilometres long, and the venue for international rowing trials. To the naturalist, shallower Whakamaru, though its power station is the centre for North Island electricity operations, is far richer in wildlife. Its abundant vegetation and swamp growth attract dabchick, grey duck, shags, innumerable croaking Australian frogs (the large green tree or golden ball species, *Litoria aurea*), white-faced herons and the usual summer complement of waterside dragonflies, red admirals and legions of twinkling blue butterflies which haunt the grasses and wild clovers of damp meadows.

Smallest hydro-electric station is Waipapa, with its little artificial lake charmingly framed between lofty, pine-clad forests. A road borders the lake, and side tributaries give glimpses of white waterfalls as you follow the Waikato north towards Cambridge and smiling paddocks of rich dairy farms. The land is smoother here, much of it recovered from ancient swamps, the former haunt of bittern, wild duck, fernbird, crakes, bog plants, and the curious native mudfish.

The Australian green tree frog, abundant throughout New Zealand today.

Two dabbling (non-diving) ducks. The grey duck *Anas superciliosa* (above) is numerous throughout all low-lying waters from the Kermadecs south to the Auckland and Campbell Islands. The sexes are alike, speckled brown, and there is a pale eye-brow stripe and the speculum panel in the wing is green, the feet olive-coloured.

The mallard *Anas platy-rhynchos* (left) introduced from Europe is spreading rapidly, both naturally and artificially as a large and highly edible duck. The female resembles the grey duck in its drab speckled plumage, but the speculum is blue and the underwing white. The male in breeding plumage is a picture of many colours. After breeding both these ducks assume a uniform, drab dress during the early autumn moult, rendering them less conspicuous. The mallard has orange-coloured feet.

93

The upstanding nikau palm *Rhopalostylis sapida* thrives in damp ground. Its red berries are devoured by birds and its young pith was once food to the Maori people.

The sulphur-crested white cockatoo, an Australian parrot with a raucous screech, escaped from captivity and now breeding wild in small numbers in New Zealand.

The Waikato is an historic river. Its fertile middle and lower reaches, navigable by small steamers, were coveted by Pakeha settlers, who brought British soldiers to wrest the best land from the resident Maori tribes. Today it is a peaceful broad river as easy to glide upon in your boat as is the Thames in the heart of England.

Many centuries ago the Waikato flowed north through an immense swamp directly to the shallow delta and arm of the Pacific which Captain Cook named the Firth of Thames. During some undefined cataclysm of land movement centuries ago, its path to the Pacific coast was blocked by upheaved hills, and the river was forced westwards to spill its floodwaters into the Tasman. Dark, tree-clad Taupiri, sacred mountain of the Waikato Maori, rises steeply some 400 m above the river at this turning-point, gazing eastwards upon the fens and bogs of the abandoned delta, a huge area known today as the Hauraki Swamp. Underneath the peat lie almost unlimited deposits of coal - another reason for Pakeha acquisition of the Waikato plains, which was the end result of the cessation of the Maori struggle to hold on to them.

In 1859 geologist von Hochstetter reported: 'Here is a treasury of buried fuel that can be extracted when European settlers spread over the fair land of the Waikato and steamboats ply the river, gateway to the interior of the North Island.' Five years later a journalist wrote in the *New Zealand Herald*: 'Where the bee now drains honey from the miles of flowery teatree, shall teem gin shops and streets rampant with the vice of great towns. The river, no more the solitary haunt of the wild duck, shall run black and filthy under bridges, bearing thousands of ships upon its ugly bosom, and under it the bodies of sin-haunted hunger-maddened suicides, whose last gaze has been upon the flare of gas.'

True, there was a coal boom around the present town of Huntly for half a century to about 1950, but production has since been controlled and reserved, and pollution of the river forbidden under strict regulations. Personally we like to explore the still extensive swamps for their wild plants and animals, although black craters of open-cast coalmining blot parts of the landscape. (We are told some farmland will be restored, and a fine recreation lake will be left in the deepest dug hole.)

We take our farewell at the mouth of the river, Port Waikato, no longer a busy trading-post and military barracks, but a pleasant, sleepy holiday village. The river here is clean, and noted for its whitebait catch. Walking along the coastal dunes, you may find, as we have, the nests of black oystercatcher and banded dotterel. In nearby limestone cliffs the splendid Australian sulphur-crested cockatoo has long been a familiar resident.

South Island rivers are shorter as they run seawards from the alpine chain, wilder, more unpredictable, subject to violent flooding from the heavy rain precipitation on the Tasman coast. The fascinating, down-to-earth story of the early colonisation of one of the longest, the Rangitata, is given in *A First Year in Canterbury Settlement* by Samuel Butler, later famous for his satire on human society in his novel *Erewhon* (anagram for Nowhere) inspired by his experiences as a settler. To those like ourselves who have followed Sam's travels along Canterbury rivers, the comparison with Then and Now is interesting. He was an observant and intelligent man. Born in 1841, educated at St John's College, Cambridge, he emigrated to New Zealand in 1865, avowedly to make his fortune, but principally to escape from his father, Canon Thomas Butler, a grim disciplinarian who nevertheless remitted him the money to set up as a sheep farmer.

On arrival at Christchurch, Sam records his amazement on hearing another (gentleman) adventurer say he was not going to wash for a year. Sam soon adopted the same terse runholder's speech, having discovered that everything revolved around sheep, which you avoided mentioning. 'If his sheep were clean, then *he* was clean. Most marvellous of all, *he* "lambs" himself.' (No reference to his ewes, for he *is* his sheep - and flockmaster.)

As Sam rode on horseback along the rivers Hurunui, Waimakariri, Rakaia, Ashburton and Rangitata in search of remote virgin land offered by the Land Office and vaguely described as 'bounded by the snowy mountains', he was also looking for signs of gold, lately discovered in Otago. He slept in the open with his saddle for pillow. 'I carried a cat on the pommel, for the rats used to take the meat from off your plate.' (Evidently the very tame kiore rat brought by the Maori.)

This wild, uninhabited high country was uninviting, naked and faded brown in the summer drought, but offering heart-lifting glimpses of the majestic heights of Mt Cook '. . . so hazardous I do not think any human being will ever reach its top'. He found no gold, but frequently came across the bones of huge moas 'lying in a heap on the ground, but never a perfect skeleton. Little heaps of their gizzard stones consist of very smooth and polished flints and cornelians, with sometimes quartz; the birds generally chose rather pretty stones.'

Sam accurately describes the black-fronted tern as 'a beautiful bird with black satin head and lavender satin and white body, orange bill and feet; and is not seen in the back country during winter.' Also on the Rangitata 'There are paradise ducks, hawks, red-bills, sandpipers and seagulls. The red-bill [South Island pied oystercatcher] is identical with the oystercatcher of the Cornish coast, with long orange bill and feet.'

Sam does not elaborate on the sandpipers, other than to say they are 'very like a lark in plumage'. At that time little was known of the unique wrybill plover which he must have seen on his frequent crossings of the Rangitata's shingle beds. Although tame, this charming little bird matches the grey-white shingle perfectly, where it sits tight upon its two or three neutrally coloured eggs, and is easily overlooked. Nor does he specifically mention the banded dotterel and stilts now breeding plentifully on these Canterbury shingle beds. The gull he saw would have been the small black-billed *Larus bulleri*, inland representative of the red-billed gull of the coast. Probably the large black-backed gull had not yet colonised - today it is a

South Island pied oyster-catcher -
artist's impressions

scavenger of sheep country, feeding on carcases and raiding the nests of the riverine birds. Nor had skylarks been imported as yet. Sam writes that 'on the plains one sees a little lark with two white feathers in the tail, in other respects exactly like the English skylark save that he does not soar, and has only a little chirrup instead of song' - a fair description of our native pipit.

The paradise duck proved useful as food. 'The male appears black, with white on the wing. He says "whiz" through his throat, and dwells a long time on the "z". If she is wounded, he will come to see what is the matter. When they have young they feign lameness, like the plover; I have several times been thus tricked.' Sam shot the old birds but found them 'very bad eating, but the eggs are excellent. We look about for the young ones, clip the top joint off one wing, and in a few months' time, we get prime young ducks for the running after them.'

Sam felt sorry for the native quail. 'It is most excellent eating. The poor thing is entirely defenceless; it cannot take more than three flights, then it is done up. Some say fires have destroyed them, my own opinion is that wild cats, which have increased so as to become very numerous, have driven the little creatures off the face of the earth.' This unique endemic quail is now extinct.

The 'woodhen' (weka, now scarce in Canterbury) intrigues Sam. 'It cannot fly but has a curious Paul-Pry-like gait which is amusing. It is incredibly bold and will come right into a house, an arrant thief. One was seen to run off with a gold watch. Another ran off with the pannikins at a camp, which were only recovered by hearing the woodhens tapping their bills against them. They are reckoned good eating by some - from fat woodhens a good deal of oil can be got, sovereign for rheumatics, wounds or bruises, for softening one's boots, and so forth. The egg, dirtily streaked and spotted a dusky purple, is the best eating I have ever tasted.'

The flightless weka or woodhen - 'a Paul-pry gait'

It was the practice of these early runholders, including first settlers Tripp and Acland, established at Mt Peel and Orari Gorge, downstream of Butler's run (which he named Mesopotamia), to burn the country to get rid of old tussock and the 'detestable Spaniard' (*Aciphylla colensoi*) with its sharp spikes pointing in all directions, menacing man and beast. 'A kind of white wax, which burns with great brilliancy, exúdes from the leaf. I have seen no grander sight than the fire upon a country that has never been burnt before. The flames roar and every now and then a glorious lurid flare marks the ignition of an Irishman [or matagouri, the almost leafless shrub *Discaria toumatou*, which is covered with long, sharp spikes].

Today you may drive comfortably along tarseal most of the way to Mesopotamia in its beautiful setting of a wide valley under the snowy mountains. We recorded several birds unknown to Butler; Canada geese are numerous, and most of the introduced finches, blackbird, song thrush, Australian magpie and skylark. We were fortunate to see a solitary white heron fishing in the Rangitata - a visitor from the only known colony of about 20 pairs nesting in Okarito lagoon on the Tasman coast due west of Mesopotamia. But Sam had also seen what he describes as 'the white crane, a beautiful bird with immense wings of purest white'. This is the kotuku of Maori legend, sacred because it has always been rare in Aotearoa, though numerous in Australia.

In Sam's day there were only 'two sorts of fish - a minnow, and an eel which grows to a great size, even in clear snow-fed rivers. They are excellent eating.' In the February month of our last visit the Rangitata was alive with fresh-run quinnat salmon, the males eagerly courting the hen fish in fast-flowing water so shallow that their fins were rippling the surface above the shingle in which the female was excavating her egg nursery or redd. This big American salmon was successfully introduced in 1875. The Rangitata sustains a large annual run, beginning in December. The mature, big-jawed males can attain weights up to 29 kg, but average one-third this size.

We observed that a few had already spawned, were losing their rosy nuptial flush and becoming emaciated, pitiful objects as they drifted downstream, dying, unable to swim upright. Good pickings for scavenging heron, harrier, gull and feral cat, in this natural recycling of the river's resources. There is a miracle here, in the migration of the young salmon parr, reared for a few years in the headwaters, to feed in the sea - no one knows exactly where - for long enough to attain those heavy weights, and then, in glistening, fine condition, swim back to the headwaters where they were born, to spawn, and then to die.

Atlantic salmon, *Salmo salar*, introduced as ova about 1870, throve as hatchlings in South Island rivers, but on migrating to feed at sea in due course, never found their way back. (Maybe they instinctively searched for their Atlantic feeding grounds, which lie off Iceland and Greenland!) Only those introduced in large deep Lakes Te Anau and Manapouri have survived, but they are lake-bound and, without the rich marine diet of sea-run fish remain small, around 2kg in weight.

OPPOSITE: The white heron *Egretta alba* is the legendary kotuku of Maori myth. Although common in Australia only about 50 individuals nest here, on the west coast of the South Island.

100

The present Mesopotamia would please Sam. It is now a substantial settlement, sheltered by plantations of native and exotic trees, where bellbirds sing. The site of the house which Sam sketched in his book is marked by a commemorative plaque fixed to the wall of his old dairy, hard by a modern school (twelve pupils at the time of our visit) for the children of local runholders and their shepherds. Runholders here operate their own small planes and helicopters in which, with luck, you may enjoy 'scenic' flights to view the magnificent back country, and look for chamois and thar along the snowline.

Red deer *Cervus elaphus*, with maturing antlers.

The High Country

Full many a glorious morning I have seen
Flatter the mountain tops with sovereign eye.
Wm Shakespeare (1564-1616)

On such a morning we first saw the silver alpine chain of Aotearoa (Land of the Long White Cloud) as our ship *Rangitoto* approached Cook Strait. A clear, calm December day, not yet midsummer, and still the snow persisting, a sparkling sunlit mantle floating high above the heat haze crowning the brown rock walls of distant Marlborough.

A heart-lifting lure and challenge! Little did we realise that within the next month we would be tramping in the sweet, sharp air of alpine flower-fells, up to the edge of melting glaciers and the snowlines of mountain peaks in several national parks in both islands: to cratered Ruapehu in the Tongariro National Park, at 2806m the highest North Island peak; to Mt Taranaki, rising 2518m from green pastures at the edge of the Tasman Sea; then long days in Tiri-tiri-o-te-Moana (Mirage of the Ocean) - the sonorous Maori name for the vast snow-capped sweep of the South Island main divide.

Had this book been written forty years ago we would have included in the list of extinct New Zealand birds a large flightless rail known to science as *Notornis mantelli* - the takahe of the Maori people, who hunted this substantial meaty bird so easily run down by their native dog. It had already been exterminated in the North Island before the arrival of Pakeha settlers. In the South Island it was rare and confined to the uninhabited mountains of the southwest. Only four specimens were in museums, the last one killed in 1898.

Dramatically, fifty years later, Dr W.R.B. Orbell, on a deer hunt in an almost inaccessible valley in the rugged Murchison mountains, 610 m above Lake Te Anau, noticed the cigarette-like droppings of a vegetarian bird which had been feeding on tussock grass. The Wildlife Service was alerted, and mounted an expedition to search for the surviving takahe in the next summer. This work has been continued each summer since. It was a special privilege for me to be invited to join the 1962 party led by Ken Miers.

It turned out to be a perfect week of fine weather, unusual in this remote, rainy high country of *Nothofagus* beech and snow tussock under glacial cirques and precipitous rock ridges. The only quick access is by float-plane from beautiful 128-kilometre-long Lake Te Anau - a twelve-minute spiral ascent to alight on

Alpine buttercup *Ranunculus haastii*

an alpine tarn, (now named Lake Orbell) in Takahe Valley, where there is a small hut, base for wildlife studies.

Typical of Fiordland mountains are these snow-fed lakes scooped out by glacial action and dammed by a moraine of boulders and gravel deposited by the melting glacier. We waded through rushes and aquatic vegetation where a lively family of a white-headed paradise duck and her downy ducklings swam away on the alarm whistle of her black drake, swooping white-winged overhead. In deeper water a crested grebe was diving with a flotilla of the dusky scaup duck (the drake has a bright golden eye) and their young - the latter comically bobbing to the surface, too buoyant to stay below for more than a few seconds. Dragonflies and damselflies darted after the troublesome sandflies, or performed their curious pairing loops in tandem under the energising sun. Near the hut a thrush sang loudly from an isolated beech, her song clear above the tinkling voices of chaffinch and redpoll. A wild and beautiful pristine paradise. High overhead three birds soared on rounded wings, circling on the thermals of rising air above the lake.

'Keas,' smiled Ken at our upwards stare. 'I'll call them down presently. They've spotted us anyway. But first a billy of tea . . .'

Somehow the door of the hut had burst open during the winter. The ever-inquisitive keas had joined with several resident wekas in dragging all that was movable into the open: boxes and bags torn open, flour, sugar and rice strewn, even tins of food dented and some pierced by stabbing beaks. As we cleaned up the mess and drank tea, the wekas peeked at us from the doorway. Suddenly, with a loud 'kee-yah' a fine mountain parrot alighted with scrabbling claws upon the tin roof, then dived down into the hut. It walked impudently to the fireplace and with the long hook of its beak began dragging sticks from the fire.

'Old Tinpot, we call him - a regular cobber each year,' said Ken. 'Not keen on bread. Prefers to lick butter. Bet you won't catch him . . .'

But later I did, by laying a trail of butter between the door and the fireplace and slamming the door shut with my climbing stick as soon as he was engrossed in licking the butter nearest the fire. He was duly leg-banded - secateur-sharp bill wrapped in my sweater - searched for parasites, and released.

'The first kea to be so distinguished,' said Ken. 'Your mana is high!'

Our task was to locate and mark the local resident takahe, some nine pairs, in both Takahe and Point Burn Valleys. Six of us walked line abreast through the spongy, knee-high vegetation around the lake, where takahe feed on the succulent basal portion and tender new blades of *Danthonia* tussock, holding each morsel in the claws of one foot to nibble it as daintily as a caged parrot.

'Sing out if you see a red topknot gliding through the tussock tops,' ordered Ken, 'and run like hell to keep it in view until we can encircle it.'

The huge scarlet bill and frontal plate - much more extensive than that of the smaller, common pukeko (swamp

Kea

Takahe

hen) - is a conspicuous advertisement to other takahe here in their misty mountain habitat. Unaccustomed to the flying rugby tackles of biologists, the adults were not difficult to run down and capture. My first captive, however, was a downy black chick still with the little yellow spike on the upper mandible used to crack open the shell when hatching. I almost trod on its crouching form. It squeaked on being picked up. Immediately its parents uttered their deep 'oomph' response, lifting their red topknots above the tussock, then making a tentative approach in defence of their child, but they were nervous, having being leg-banded in a previous summer. They too were caught, their ring numbers, weight, state of moult, feather parasites and other data recorded, and the trio released.

'Not rapturously handsome,' my diary notes. 'The massive beak makes for a top-heavy appearance, but any bird so close to extinction has a special quality when held in your arms! The dark plumage is silky, gleaming with irridescent blues and greens, the long narrow feathers resembling a cockerel's shining hackles. No visible wings. Big scarlet feet. Plump too. Adults weigh up to 9 kg. - a substantial meal for a hungry predator. If only they can be saved and bred in captivity - like turkeys?'

In that joyful week of fine weather we explored the hinterland of gloriously wild Murchison high country A few takahe still had unhatched eggs. Two (at most) are laid in a bower of tussock. Shared incubation lasts one month. The

Takahe and pukeko. Note the heavier bill and frontal shield in the takahe (left).

Anthus novaeseelandiae, New Zealand pipit at nest.

precocious chick is taught early to feed itself, guarded and warmed at intervals by affectionate parents. During the long winter the family remains together, retreating during snow to feed on fern and other roots under the canopy of the beech forest of the escarpment.

Like the red deer we encountered (now a competitor of the takahe for the most nutritious tussock and sapling tree food), some takahe families walk up the steep forested escarpment to the open fell-field above the treeline, to browse alpine meadows of snow tussock where the air is cool and fewer blood-sucking flies exist. We found the deer (some wapiti among the red) segregated into stag parties, or hinds with fawns; all bounded away on our approach. We saw few birds save the ubiquitous tame keas (no sheep farmer to shoot them in this sheep-free high country) flicking their scarlet underwings and searching the rock outcrops for items of their varied diet. We found a nest of the native pipit when the owner fluttered from a niche under a clump of speargrass in a fell garden of alpine flowers.

The New Zealand pipit feeds as it runs rapidly along the ground, snapping up food, chasing winged insects. The male has a brief needling song, uttered, after a short ascent skywards, as it descends on parachuting wings. It is often seen on dusty gravel roads in hilly country, and can be mistaken for a skylark, having the same brown and buff plumage and white outer tail feathers. The pipit lacks the lark's crest, is more slender, and its long tail is constantly wagged up and down, both when walking and standing. The lark's incomparable torrent of song pours down from high in the sky, especially above open level farmland. The pipit is now confined to nesting in more rural areas.

Our pipit adapts admirably to the harsh winters where it is resident on sub-Antarctic islands. Here Man is rare and this bird extremely tame; like the fantail, it will flutter around your feet in search of disturbed insects. When winter snows lie over the land, the pipit finds sufficient food along the tidal shore down to the low-water zone where the giant kelp is rich in marine organisms.

European skylark *Alauda arvensis*

Thar, a large, shaggy, russet-brown Himalayan species of goat, were a gift of the Duke of Bedford from his wild animal collection at Woburn Abbey in England. From a nucleus introduced in 1904 at Mt Cook, they have spread to cover the whole alpine chain, in summer inhabiting the highest crags where there is any vegetation, and descending to about 1200m in the depth of winter. In this habitat our first glimpse of a flock was from the ski-plane circling to land on the Franz Joseph glacier. Both thar and chamois can be viewed at close quarters in semi-wild conditions at several 'wild animal' parks, notably at the deer farm near Frankton, located on a rocky hill which offers spectacular views to Queenstown and Lake Wakatipu. In the wild the thar flock is divided for much of the year: the mature, heavily-maned bulls, 1 m at shoulder height and up to 90 kg in weight - the much sought-after target of sportsmen - form small groups of five to twenty, until rutting time in April-May. Six months later the nannies give birth to one, sometimes twin, kids as spring returns to their rocky nursery and

the snow begins to melt, revealing the tender buds of the alpine flora.

About half the bulk and weight of thar, chamois are natives of European and Asian alps. For their handsome appearance, golden brown in summer with dark facial stripe between the sharply pointed ears and muzzle, black legs and short upright horns curved backwards at the tops to form semicircular hooks, they were considered 'royal' beasts, being also a challenge to hunt, good to eat, and providing buckskin. In 1907 the Emperor of Austria presented two males and six females to the New Zealand Government. Released near the Hermitage, Mt Cook, they have now spread along the whole South Island alpine chain, from Fiordland to the Kaikoura ranges, to high cliffs above the sea east of Blenheim. Extremely nimble and sure-footed, their agility in their precipitous terrain is helped by the hoof having a hard edge with a soft centre pad, providing an ideal non-slip grip on rock. Of necessity they are diurnal, sleeping all night.

Chamois have large eyes, and rely much on long sight to detect the distant approach of enemies. They vanish from the landscape - as many hunters have been disappointed to discover - on sighting a man with a gun, yet where they have been given complete protection in some European parks we have visited, notably in southern Switzerland, chamois flocks allow a quiet approach within about 200 m. Like thar, but more gregariously, chamois form distinct sexual groups: adult billies, and nannies with kids and yearlings. The billies spar among themselves for as many nannies as they can keep in hand during the April rut, the weaker males retiring and becoming solitary for a while. Only one kid is born, at the end of the year. Overpopulation and insufficient control of chamois in New Zealand has resulted in overbrowsing of the alpine fell-field, with some malnutrition and accompanying diseases in the flocks (scab, conjunctivitis). In hard winters hungry chamois may come down into high-country farmland; they have even been seen looking for food on the outskirts of small towns.

PRECEDING PAGES: Rock wrens (male on left) - smallest birds of the alpine winter world.

Two curious high country inhabitants. The 'vegetable sheep' *Raoulia rubra* (above) and the stinkhorn fungus with spore stage fully erupted and a dying fruit body.

A dreaming place to be at midsummer - to stand and stare awhile on the sunlit crags amid alpine flowers, kea cries and thin pipit song in our ears, and before us away to the northwest, ridge after ridge of brown-green heights stretching to the snow mantle of Mt Aspiring's lofty peak, 3035 m.

The fell-field is the permanent habitat of the tiny rock wren, which has a thin, piping song like that of the pipit. For those who do not climb strenuously, this golfball-sized bird (almost tailless) can be watched with patience from the few mountain pass roads over the main divide of the South Island. Near the Homer Tunnel above Milford we have found the nest of this restless little endemic, with its habit of bobbing each time it alights. This nest was a substantial ball of dry grass with a side entrance, domed against the weather, and tucked under a mossy boulder, virtually impossible to locate if one of the owners had not appeared with a grasshopper in its bill. When its mate flitted from low scrub carrying a grub and crossed the road in the same direction, we followed. As these birds bobbed a curtsey from the boulder there was time to note the comparatively long legs, toes and claws, adapted to grip firmly the rock and ice of its windy habitat. Other than skiing visitors, few see this scrap of life in winter, but somehow it survives and thrives for more than half the year in the sub-zero temperature of its chosen habitat, feeding on dormant insects and the berries of mountain plants in the shelter of alpine scrub.

Back at Takahe Valley hut, Old Tinpot got his revenge for our rough handling earlier, by dancing all night on the corrugated-iron roof, tapping with sharp claws and bill. He appeared never to sleep, and seemed keen to ensure that we did not either. Anyway, there was so much going on in the brief midsummer midnight: ruru (morepork) owls cooed 'quoor-ruru' mournfully, kiwis yodelled, wekas chorused, kea and kaka uttered their onomatopoeic Maori-given names, by which native birds are popularly known.

Our morning bathe, naked in the chill, tumbling cascades of the burn from Lake Orbell, was watched with tame indifference by a family of blue mountain duck, squatting endearingly together on a boulder in mid-torrent. We admired the dove-blue sheen of the upper parts, and the apron of tawny polka-dots of the breast of the adults. Now and then four pied ducklings nimbly leapt in and out of the rapids, already expert in diving for their breakfast of caddis worms and other aquatic insects, staying in the smooth lee of the boulder to avoid being swept downstream.

The tameness of birds in these mountains is due to their inexperience of man as a predator. Even the Maori people, arriving from their tropical isle (the traditional Hawaiki), shunned the cold mountain land of the southwest. Only under pressure of increasing population did the weaker tribes penetrate as far as the eastern half of the South Island, which was rich in gigantic moas. These they exterminated long before the white man set foot on Aotearoa. As Captain Cook reported, cannibalism was the Maori answer to overpopulation, and fear of it drove the weaker tribes to eke out an existence in remote, inhospitable regions. Cook describes in 1777 how during a sojourn in Dusky Sound (some 75 km from Takahe Valley) he encountered an isolated stone-age Maori family subsisting on birds, fish and seals. He gave them presents of 'hatchets and spike nails' - their first contact with the Age of Metal. Subsequently, when Vancouver visited Dusky Sound in 1794 the natives had disappeared, confirming Cook's surmise that they were a wandering fugitive group of hunters.

Apropos of these facts of history, Ken Miers took us to a cave in the limestone bluffs of Takahe Valley where he and Robert Falla, while looking for kakapo dens in 1949, found the bones and feathers of a small forest moa (possibly of the last moa in the world) with the evidence that it had been roasted and eaten by a Maori hunting party. The cave contained tussock beds, a fire-rubbing stick, a flaxen sandal and other signs of temporary occupation. One moa bone had a series of deep incisions which could only have been made with a metal knife, and therefore could be dated not earlier than Captain Cook's visit in 1777. The moa could have been carved up later - perhaps during the intensive Pakeha sealing operations along the Fiordland coast which began about 1803.

We found plenty of the round balls of old kakapo dung in 'Moa Cave' and other dry holes along the foot of the bluff, indefinitely preserved by the limestone dust. We had listened in vain each night for the booming of the male kakapo, once

Profile and leg studies of the kakapo, the world's largest parrot.

numerous in Fiordland, and a source of food to early Pakeha explorers. All we could discover were a few plant-browsed trails of this flightless, nocturnal parrot, trails which are recognisable because they pass *under* ground cover and low branches; deer trails in the bush were open to man's height, and well marked with hoof slots.

The female kakapo in her nesting burrow is extremely vulnerable to four-footed predators during the many lone weeks she attends to the incubation of her two to four white eggs, and the brooding and rearing of her helpless downy chicks. The male is concerned only to attract a female ready to mate to his territory on a hill ridge. This he does by excavating a bowl in the ground as a sounding box for his explosive release of air from his inflated lungs, resulting in a drumming boom carrying far from

Kakapo feathers

this vantage point. Since our visit this beautiful large, moss-green parrot has become extinct on the mainland. A few old males, booming in vain, may yet survive on Stewart Island, where flightless birds are troubled by feral cats and rats. Just in time some females and males have been trans-shipped to the ideal refuge of the rain-forest of cat-free Little Barrier Island.

High country forest in the South Island is still a main stronghold of arboreal native birds. The yellowhead and brown creeper warblers are unique to the South Island. Robin and tomtit in these forests have yellow breasts - the North Island subspecies are white waistcoated. There are cuckoos, tui, riflemen, grey warbler, bellbird, silver-eye, pigeon, fantail, falcon and parakeets in goodly numbers in these majestic fastnesses of evergreen beech and other native trees.

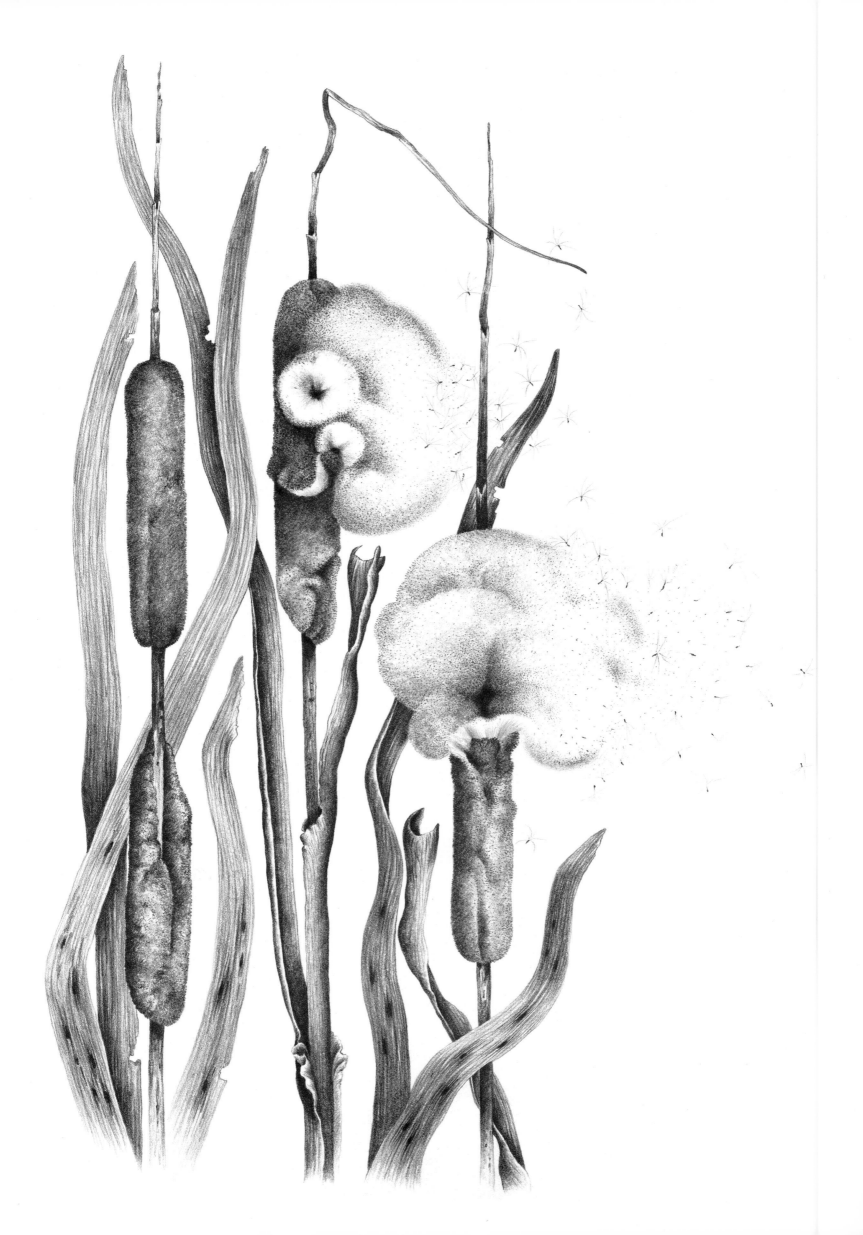

Many Lakes

I will arise and go now, for always night and day
I hear lake water lapping, with low sounds by the shore;
While I stand on the roadway, or on the pavements gray,
I hear it in the deep heart's core.

W.B. Yeats (1865-1939)

A 'delightfully watery country - all these hundreds of lakes and rivers!' exclaimed a visiting fly-fisherman, demanding that we take him to 'that world mecca of trout-fishing, Lake Taupo. And how sensible - anyone can fish anywhere, it seems, for the price of a licence costing only a couple of bucks.'

Taupo, largest and deepest of North Island lakes, is comparatively young, formed as the result of an immense volcanic explosion about 3800 BC, which smothered the immediate landscape with hills of pumice and a mantle of ash. The blast destroyed all fauna and flora therein, and set fire to more distant forest. Long· before the first Polynesian settlers arrived about AD 750, the pristine forests - tall cathedrals of giant kahikatea, totara, rimu, matai and miro - were fully re-established. These people, who became the Maori, were seafarers living at first along the coast. It was some years before, following rivers inland, they discovered and inhabited the thermal areas around Lakes Rotorua and Taupo, with their magic hot pools, geysers and sulphuric vents.

Our earliest memories of these thermal lakes are of a Maori family wading and diving in the narrow winding Ohau channel where the waters of Lake Rotorua flow into picturesque Lake Rotoiti, lying about one metre lower. They were seeking the koura, the tasty freshwater crayfish (*Paranephrops*). This miniature lobster is about 12 cm when adult, excluding the pincer claws which - another vivid memory - can give you a sharp nip. One warm evening, cooling off in a tepid pool under trees on the edge of Lake Taupo, half-submerged and half-asleep, we were rudely awakened by a large, greenish-looking koura nibbling the flesh of our naked toes. No blood drawn, but both marine and freshwater crayfish are scavengers of dead fish and other animal casualties, including drowned humans.

Around boat wharves the koura is easily captured if you lower a fragment of fish or meat tied to a string into the water. In the clear water of Lake Taupo you may watch koura emerge from the dark shelter of wooden piles and approach the bait with sensitive whiskers and stalked eyes assessing its edibility. Give it

Larger than the white-faced heron, the bittern, *Botaurus poiciloptilus*, is chiefly a twilight and nocturnal feeder, skulking in raupo cover by day. During the summer evenings its loud, booming 'woomp' advertises its presence at a nesting territory.

OPPOSITE: Raupo dispersing seed

117

time to fasten tightly upon the morsel and become engrossed in feeding then you may draw it slowly on the baited string towards the surface, taking care to insert your landing net beneath before the crayfish is aware of the peril of capture.

The Ohau Maori were catching a quantity of koura by their traditional method of fastening a small, leafy shrub to the bed of the channel. Left overnight, this becomes inhabited by koura seeking cover against the coming daylight. It is then cautiously lifted until the net can be inserted underneath. As the bush breaks the surface, the alarmed koura shoot downwards, tail first - fastest method of retreat for all shrimp-like crustaceans - into the net.

Other species of *Paranephrops* inhabit South and Stewart Island rivers, ponds and lakes. Freshwater crayfish are found world-wide in temperate and subtropical waters. As children we sought them in English streams, and have since found them in quite small rivulets in Samoa and Fiji. How they originally colonised remote volcanic islands is unknown. The fertile female carries many hundreds of eggs attached to the swimmerets under her body, protected by her flexible tail. These hatch and float away as free-swimming plankton. As they grow they can only increase body size by casting off their old shell, - complete even to the joints of their legs, swimmerets and whiskers, as a glove is withdrawn from the hand. Prior to this moult the koura accumulates a reservoir of lime in its intestines as the source for building up its next suit of armour. Until this new shell hardens the koura must hide from predators in some underwater hole.

The empty, oval shells of the freshwater mussel (*Hyridella* spp.), another edible shellfish - prized of old by the Maori as a cure for child ailments - are frequently seen on lakeside and riverbanks. The upper surface is rough, dark green, but the under surface is a decorative pearl white. Few of us encounter the living mussel unless we dive or wade deep to its dwelling place, half buried in mud. Here it feeds by filtering water through two siphons, one inhalant, the other exhalant. The adult reproduces a quantity of eggs, which hatch into perfect shelled miniatures, pass out through the exhalant tube and become part of the plankton and in danger of being swept away by currents - if in a river - to the sea. However, each larval mussel has an extensible filament, sensitive to the presence of small fish or other moving creatures, even a koura. A series of minute hooks around the rim of the tiny shell enable the infant mussel to attach firmly to the tough scales or armour of the host. Thus secured and protected, the young mussel hitches a joyride, benefitting from scraps of leftover organic food from its host's meals. After a few months the juvenile mussel has grown sufficiently to drop off at the right moment and anchor itself permanently in a suitable mud habitat.

The primitive mudfish (*Neochanna* spp.) has a curious life cycle. It normally inhabits the still water of lakes, ponds and swamps, often hidden by aquatic vegetation. When the water-level sinks during drought it follows it downward, wriggling deep into the mud with the disapppearing moisture. It has been found a metre deep in this soft mud. Here it aestivates (summer hibernates) for weeks, even months. It is very fat from earlier feeding and can stand a long fast. When the water floods back with autumn rains it emerges to feast on aquatic larvae, and land insecs drowned in the flood. This is the hour of liberation: the mature fish come together at the surface in a frantic mating. The males shed their milt as the female splatters her eggs in all directions, even upon the land. The eggs hatch immediately and the tiny fish seek cover in wet ground. They are carried away by rain and flood to establish new colonies in other pools.

The primitive mudfish. It is said that when early settlers found mudfish among their potato crops in low-lying paddocks, they wrote home to praise the productivity of New Zealand soil which produced a harvest of fish and potatoes at one digging!

The elegant black swan, *Cygnus atratus,* was first introduced from Australia in 1864 as a handsome ornamental waterfowl rather than an edible sporting bird. (Young cygnets may be tender, but adult swans are unappetising and tough.) It has since spread to colonise most lakes, large ponds and estuaries. It does not dive, but the long neck assists in plucking aquatic rooted plants. It freely eats seaweed, and waddles ashore to crop grass if hungry. Four to seven cygnets are raised annually in a good season of sufficient food. Where numerous, the swan nests colonially. One of the largest concentrations (possibly in the world) has been at Lake Ellesmere, a brackish lagoon south of Christchurch. We first saw this in 1962, when it was estimated that some 50,000 black swans were nesting; they had in

fact become a nuisance to local farmers by overgrazing their paddocks. They were being controlled by collecting their eggs (40,000 sold annually) and by interfering with their nests.

By 1968 they had multiplied to 80,000 breeding adults. In that year occurred a terrible storm in which the inter-island ferry *Wahine* capsized as it entered Wellington Harbour, with great loss of human lives. In the same hurricane the Lake Ellesmere weed beds were swept away in one night, depriving the swans of their normal food supply. Seventy-five percent subsequently died of starvation and the diseases of malnutrition. After a year or more of virtual non-breeding at Lake Ellesmere, the swans (and the weed) have been slow to recover. A Wildlife Service estimate gave only 200 cygnets

reared in 1978; they may have doubled that number at Ellesmere by now. The New Zealand population overall is settling down to a slower rate of reproduction in keeping with the food supply, and because of a longer non-breeding period before finding and taking up suitable nesting territory for the first time. Such is Nature's way of regulating population by the amount of nourishing food available.

In its native Australia, when the waters of shallow lakes evaporate during a long drought, this swan solves the food problem by migrating to reach areas of more recent rainfall with shallow feeding lakes and lagoons. Brackish water inland or by the sea is acceptable, provided it has pastures of *zostera* or other edible salt-tolerant plants.

Water life quickens as lake temperatures rise with spring sunlight. In quiet shallows green algae reproduces, rapidly filming the water with the opaque nutrient nekton, basic vegetable feed for millions of microscopic water animals whose beauty or strangeness can only be appreciated under an enlarging glass. Heavy rain, depositing a layer of cold water on the surface, causes the algae to sink to the bottom. It is devoured by young tadpoles, snails and certain fish.

In some shallow lakes submerged exotic plants have increased alarmingly, as at Lakes Rotorua and Rotoiti, where by late summer *Elodea* and *Lagarosiphon* spp., the so-called oxygen weeds, develop huge beds of trailing stems which foul fishing lines and boat propellors. Effective control is impossible; these prolific plants, which are able to re-root if chopped up, thrive on nutrient effluent from farms and sewage plants around the lakes. Spraying is far too costly and would contaminate the trout for which these lakes are famous. In such lakes black swans have greatly increased, helping to reduce the weed slightly. Periodically Nature takes a hand - exceptionally severe gales cause violent wave action, resulting in most of the mature oxygen weed being uprooted and thrown ashore to lie in massive rotting heaps.

Black swan cygnets

OVER PAGE: The lakeside habitat with Canada geese, mallard, black swan and raupo cover.

The freshwater food chain builds up from simple algae and primitive aquatic plants grazed by minute vegetarian plankton, in turn devoured by carnivorous planktonic animals: hydra (half plant, half animal, it has sting cells), tiny crustaceans, copepods, freshwater crabs, water fleas, shrimps, fish lice, worms, flukes, leeches, the nymphs and larvae of flies. Weedy lakes suit some of the introduced non-sporting coarse fish. Carp, including goldfish, are largely vegetarian, the Chinese or grass carp wholly so, but their presence is resented by the trout-fishing fraternity, who unreasonably fear that they may devour *all* the weed, which, after all, is useful cover in moderation for trout and trout food - koura, bullies, smelt, fly larvae, worms, snails, etc. Thus Man himself, the world's greatest predator, and meddler with Nature, lords it (or thinks he does) at the top of the food chain, dominating all.

Favourite food of the introduced trout and salmon parr are the submarine nymphs (pupae) of damsel flies and dragonflies. Most conspicuous of these is *Uropetela carovei*, a handsome gold- and black-banded dragonfly 8 cm long. Popularly known as the 'Devil's darning needle', from its wasp-like colouring and high-speed darting flight, creating the erroneous belief that it can sting as viciously as a wasp, this dragonfly does fly fast enough to snap up other winged insects, which it crushes in its powerful jaws. Another folklore belief was that it could sew up the ears of a scold or gossip!

The eyes of dragonflies and damselflies have up to 2800 omnatidia (lenses), providing accurate all-round vision for locating their prey, or a mate. After, and sometimes during, their curious mating ritual already described (*page 86*) the female drops her eggs as she hovers over the water. The resulting larvae may live for several years, feeding voraciously on aquatic insects and small fish, and even spiders and littoral insects, which are seized as they pass near the entrance to a submarine tunnel in which the nymph lies in wait. This is usually situated level with the water surface touching the land. When ready to leave the water, the mature nymph crawls up the nearest vegetation to reach the warm sunlight early one summer morning. The outer skin splits open and for a while the emergent soft body of the adult fly, awaiting the full expansion of its gauzy wings, is at considerable risk of being devoured by a bird or leaping fish.

South Island lakes are principally the result of earlier earth movements along the Alpine Fault, and later of surface sculpting by ice during the advances and retreats of four glacial epochs in the last 100,000 years. Several have been enlarged today for hydro-electric water storage, with consequent unnatural fluctuation of water levels which produce a stony, barren terrain during each dry spell almost devoid of interest to the naturalist.

We drove our visiting Izaak Walton - Richard Adams - to several lakes noted for their fly-fishing. Our first trip was to Lake Sumner State Forest Park, in a landrover courteously supplied by the North Canterbury Acclimatisation Society, with Field Officer Ross to guide us. It was high summer along the Hurunui River, where golden kowhai blossom had lately made way for the silver of flowering manuka, that 'rescue' shrub-tree that springs up wherever man has felled indigenous forest. In this mixed bush of manuka and decaying red and silver beech a sprinkling of native birds sang; bellbird and tui loudly, robin, tomtit and riro-riro on a softer note. Presently beautiful Lake Sumner opened out before us, with the yellow and dun screes of Mt Longfellow (1987m) rising above green beech along the shore.

While Richard fly-fished for and caught two medium-sized Sumner brown trout, we attempted a census of lake birds, and listed the flora. Flocks of Canada geese and paradise ducks are today typical of this lake in upland country, nesting secretively and singly. They are not popular with the few runholders who are unable to keep them from grazing isolated back-country paddocks of lucerne and turnips grown for hay and winter fodder. These large waterfowl become flightless during the late summer moult, and wisely take refuge on these remote lakes, where runholders, using boats, find it difficult to herd them ashore during battues intended to reduce their growing numbers.

ABOVE: The native scaup or black teal *Aythya novaeseelandiae* is a diving duck, abundant on all large lakes.

LEFT: Introduced from North America the handsome Canada goose *Branta canadensis* has found the mountain lakes and grassland ideal breeding and feeding sanctuary, and has increased almost to plague numbers.

Mallard head studies

Surprisingly, there were numerous rabbits keeping the lakeside and hill sward closely grazed, conducive to a fine coloured display of midsummer flowers, chiefly introduced species: foxglove, poppy, clovers, buttercups, mullein, marguerites, viper's bugloss, hawkweeds, centaury, and our favourite yarrow. In the mossy shade of beeches, we found greenhood and other orchids we could not name, innumerable toadstools, the curious strawberry and birdnest fungi, up-standing pale greenish cup-lichen *Cladonia*, and other wondrously bright blue, coral and silver algal plants on rocks; the ground was yellow with club moss.

We adjourned to nearby Lake Shepherd for a delicious billy of tea brewed over a stick fire by the ever-helpful Ross. He told us that Lake Shepherd was a no-shooting wildlife reserve, and of this the wildfowl seemed well aware. On this small, enchanting lake with its ample cover of raupo and reeds we counted, in round figures: 400 paradise ducks, 50 Canada geese, 20 black swans, 100 each of native grey duck and scaup (diving teal), also a few European mallard, New Zealand shoveler and Australian grey teal. A family of two adult and two young crested grebes were diving near the raupo. Black-fronted terns hawked after mosquitoes and probably mayflies, clumsily imitated by black-billed gulls with less success. Two black-backed gulls had come to drink and bathe after feeding on a sheep carcase.

The beautiful crested grebe, found almost world-wide, is confined in New Zealand to high country lakes, preferably with good raupo cover in which they build their raft nests. They are the most aquatic of birds, fly and dive well, but, with feet far to the rear of the body, they can hardly walk at all.

Of land birds, pipit, harrier and magpie were typical of this open country with its sparse, scattered clumps of flax, cabbage tree *Cordyline* spp., nikau palm, niggerhead *Carex secta*, and other rushes. In wet hollows a carpet of *Drosera auriculata*, the insect-trapping sundew, lay feasting, we hoped, on the abundant sandflies which troubled Richard.

Our visitor was still engrossed in trying the different fly lures previously discussed with Ross for this lake particularly, but to us reminiscent of Izaak Walton's advice in his immortal *The Compleat Angler*, which was first published in 1653. Walton recommends certain aquatic flies - also found in New Zealand, although they may be specifically distinct: the stonefly, the blackfly (larva known as the 'black creeper' or 'toe biter', for obvious reasons), the greendrake and duns (mayflies of many sorts), and caddis flies of several species whose larvae dress up in sundry protective adopted or manufactured clothes - a hollow twig, silken tunnel, tubes of bits of sand glued together - or simply hide under stones. All emerge as perfect insects, in thousands, to indulge their brief aerial nuptial dances above the water. It was at the end of the eighth hour that day that Richard triumphantly hooked, netted and grassed a 5 kg brown trout.

Of the many introduced fish, brown trout *Salmo trutta*, are considered to be the most thoroughly acclimatised sporting species, maintaining their numbers in all large lakes and rivers south of Auckland without artificial help. They freely enter the sea, and find their own way into unstocked lakes and rivers, but they need cool upland streams in which to spawn, and do not maintain a permanent population when introduced in the warm small lakes and streams of Northland. Rainbow trout, *Salmo gairdnerii*, are less adaptable. They were first introduced about a hundred years ago, from North American rivers, and have settled well in the larger lakes of the central North Island. They are primarily lake fish, and do not survive long naturally in cold, South Island rivers, where acclimatisation societies need to restock frequently from their hatcheries.

Lake-living trout spawn in upland tributary rivers, rainbow somewhat later than brown trout, thereby sometimes disturbing the nursery redds, filled with fertilised ova, dug by the brown trout. After spawning, the adult rainbows, referred to as 'kelts' or 'slabs', like spent salmon drift down towards the lake in emaciated condition. Few recover to spawn in a second season. Brown trout, however, may spawn for several seasons in succession, especially if they have fed in the sea. They also attain greater weights, up to 17 kg; maximum weight for the rainbow is half that size. In appearance the two species are alike; out of the water the rainbow is usually more heavily pink and cream flushed and spotted on the upper parts, fins and tail. Both are carnivorous, young parr taking insect larvae below and midges and mayfly at the surface, and small fish, koura and frogs when adult.

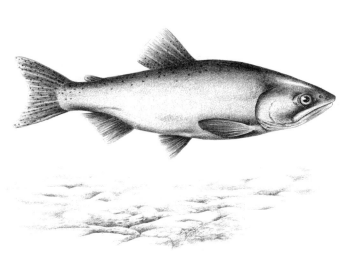

Sock-eye salmon

Brown trout with lake body pattern.

The Tidal Shore

There is a rapture on the lonely shore,
There is society, where none intrudes
By the deep sea, and music in its roar.
Lord Byron (1788-1824)

Ocean winds sweep their pure, ozone-laden air across the whole of our isolated islands; the nearest land mass, Australia, is 1600 kilometres westwards. No place in New Zealand is more than 100 kilometres from the sea, yet north to south the three main islands span some 1600 kilometres of longitude. If we try to measure the actual coastline with its innumerable bays, indentations and islands, we may find it stretches well over 12,000 kilometres in length. More to our good fortune, relatively little of our accessible shore is as yet spoiled by housing and building development, or heavy industry with its threat of pollution.

We are a young maritime nation of small population, our few cities - likeliest source of pollution - fortunately subject today to strict regulations against discharging toxic waste into the sea, river or lake. In colonial days more than a century ago it was not so. Then our population was under half a million and there were few roads. In 1872 novelist Anthony Trollope, inspector of post office management in Britain, anxious to see the 'famous hot springs' of the Rotorua lakes, was obliged to proceed by ship from Auckland to Tauranga, and thence on horseback some fifty miles inland to reach Ohinemutu and the Pink and White Terraces.

It was access by sea in small sailing vessels that enabled immigrants to establish their coastal settlements the length of our more sheltered eastern seaboard. Many of these first trading posts were too shallow as harbours for larger ships, but it was customary to beach cargo boats at high tide, for unloading into carts at low tide. With the advent of roads and motor transport, the small tidal creeks were abandoned. Today there is little sign of their once picturesque activity - perhaps a rotting wooden wharf, a derelict quarry, a rusted shell-crushing plant (as at Miranda on the Firth of Thames, now a bird sanctuary) which produced lime for building and the land. Long may these remain so for our quiet enjoyment and for the future delight of our children, who will cherish this scenic heritage of a seashore reverted to nature.

We are drawn to the elemental frontier of the ocean by the diversity of its land forms, derived in conflict (breaking down) or

The handsome, variably coloured gecko, *Hoplodactylus pacificus,* blinks sleepily in the sun. This Pacific gecko has no doubt feasted on hoppers and other nocturnal small life of the strand-line. In season it eats berries, and is found far inland in the North Island.

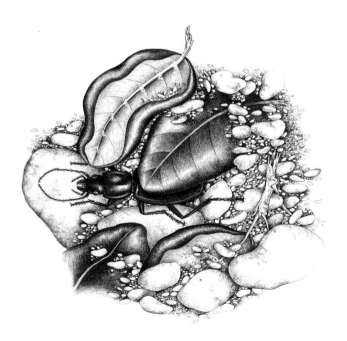

Ctenognathus novaezealandica, one of the many native ground beetles, is at home under the debris of the high-water strand-line.

co-operation (building up) with wind, water and wave action. We enjoy the freedom of movement on large and small beaches, with their glittering restlessness of twice-daily ebb and flow of the tides under the pull of the moon. (Incidentally, lunar time day, by which marine organisms live, is approximately an hour longer than the 24-hour 'sun day' of land-based fauna and flora.) Geologists delight in the visible stratification of sedimentary, volcanic, granitic and fossil-yielding calcareous layers of rock exposed in coastal cliffs, caves and rock platforms, which speak of epochs when the world was young. They enjoy examining the nature and origin of pebbles, and of sea sand composed of fine or coarse particles of disintegrated shell or sand ever on the move under the pressure of tidal currents and storm waves.

At lowest tide beachcombing Maori and Pakeha wade waist-deep in the surf, naked toes probing and sensitive to the presence of edible shellfish which live a few centimetres below the surface of wet sand or mud and feed by thrusting fine tentacles into the water to gather the almost invisible free-swimming plankton and diatoms. Such bivalves as the cockle (*Tawera* spp.), and three *Amphidesma* - the small pipi, the larger tuatua and the much larger meaty toheroa - whose empty shells are scattered on every beach, often make up long white banks in sheltered bays. Shellfish were a principal stand-by food of the coast-dwelling Maori in pre-Pakeha centuries.

In deeper water one may dive at low tide for the delicately flavoured free-swimming tipa (scallop) which has a row of rudimentary eyes. Another favourite is the paua, a univalve related to the abalone of California, with the same brilliantly irridescent shell. It can be collected at lowest tide where it clings tenaciously under stones and boulders. Its powerful muscles make it tough to eat, for which reason it should be pounded (in a cloth) for several minutes before cooking. Grilled like a steak, it is delicious.

The sea gives up its treasures and secrets where flotsam becomes jetsam, forming a strand-line accumulation of natural debris: tree branches and logs; far-travelled driftwood festooned with long-stalked goose barnacles; seaweeds, shells, carapaces and claws of crabs and crayfish; jellyfish; the peacock-blue stinging man-ó-war, *Physalia*; the by-the-wind sailor, *Velella*; seeds of many sorts; and green, free-floating capsules of mangrove, *Avicennia,* shed where this shrub grows in frost-free salt lagoons and meandering rivers north of lattitude approximately 38° south. The list is endless, including the unwelcome exuviae of human waste - bottles, plastic, waste oil, etc. Weak neap tides successively mark the beach with their strand-lines, but all are swept clean to the top of the beach by the high spring tides over new and full moon.

Storm waves at such tides push the strand-line well above the high-water mark, creating a permanent tangle of decaying organic matter exploited by a fascinating fauna and flora adapted to its warm, salty, moist micro-climate. Roll over a log to discover a world of rubbish-eaters: slaters fold up into armoured balls or run for cover; shrimp-like hoppers bounce away instinctively seawards - they feed on the beach debris at night.

Flotsam of the strand-line

131

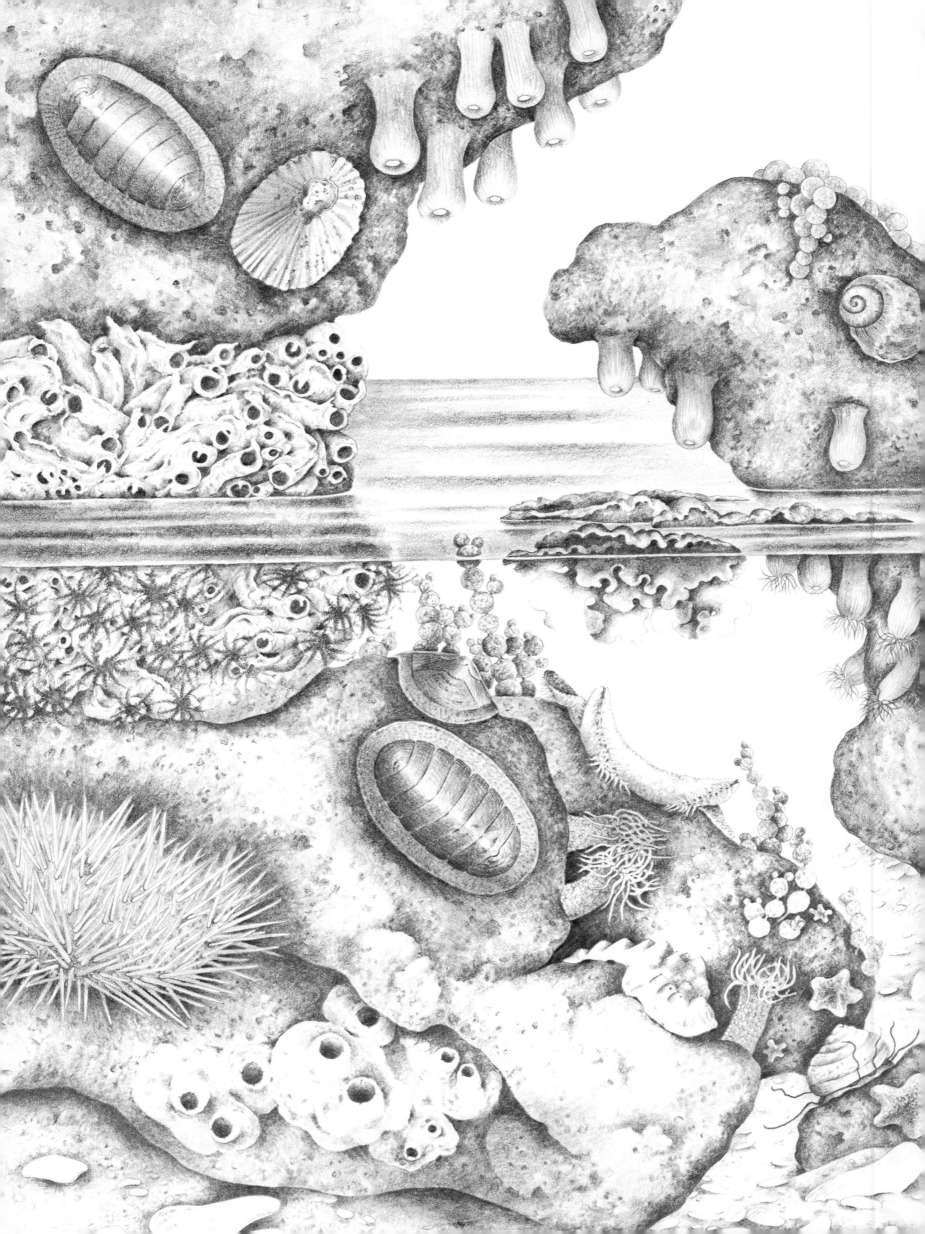

PRECEDING PAGES: Artist's impression of a rock pool with sea lettuce, cats'eyes, chiton limpet, mussel, anenome, tubeworms, sea urchin, acorn barnacle and Venus's necklace.

Clusters of the large green mussel, *Mytilus canaliculus*, attach naturally to rocks, wooden piles and other static objects submerged below the low-tide line. Popular as a table delicacy, this bivalve is also grown commercially on ropes anchored and buoyed in the sheltered waters of clean harbours and sounds. An extract of this mussel is marketed as a cure for rheumatism.

The rock pool which traps a half-metre or so of sea over low tide invites contemplation of its marine riches from a comfortable position above. Vivid white or pink sea-anemones wave their rosettes of fleshy tentacles ready to fasten upon the incautious shrimp or small fish swimming too close. Once paralysed by the anemone's poison 'sting' these captives are delivered whole into the large central stomach; indigestible parts are later disgorged. The mason worm feeds in a similar fashion, waving its tentacles to induce currents and draw planktonic life within grasping range. Its tapering body can be withdrawn into a protective case (like that of the caddis worm of the mountain streams) which the worm builds of particles of sand or shell cemented together. Another tubeworm *Vermilia* forms colonies of individual cells cemented together coral fashion, a honeycomb from which each worm projects its feeding fans. You may also find a pioneer vermilia as a single tube in a rock pool.

Sea urchins, densely covered with long, flexible dark spines, move about on these and retractile tubular 'feet'. They absorb food through the large circular opening under the body which is the mouth, complete with bony jaws. When swollen with eggs, the genital apparatus is a five-segmented orange-coloured arrangement. In this condition the soft interior of the sea urchin is considered a delicacy, eaten raw by the seafood connoisseur.

Where rivers discharge their silt to mingle with the deposits of shell and rock sand, broad mudflats are formed, rich in disintegrated vegetable and animal matter and mineral salts.

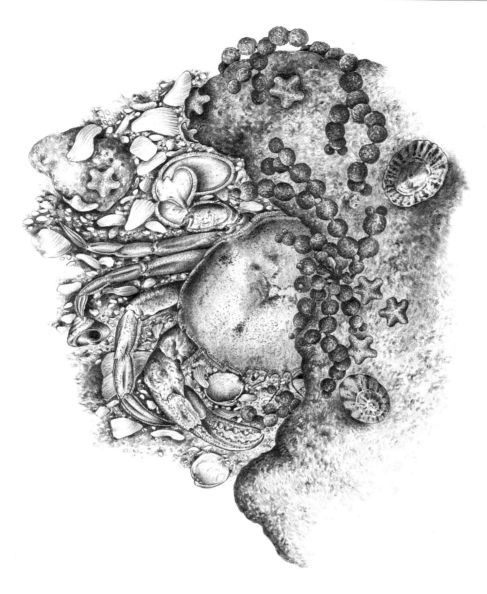

This fertile matrix forms a basic part of the marine food chain whether buried in the mud, on the surface, or floating with the tide. In sheltered salt lagoons, algae grow on the mud surface or float free in tidal pools warmed by the summer sun. Mud snails *Amphibola* proliferate by the thousand as they devour this greenish slime rich in chloryphyll. Our local Maoris still value this little snail as a food delicacy when lightly boiled; herons, kingfishers and gulls eat them sparingly, when other food is short perhaps.

These birds prefer the mud crab which abounds on all sheltered mudflats. With rapid alternative movements of its pair of pincer claws, this crab conveys algae and other minute organic matter to its mouth. It must ingest a vast proportion of mud in this hurried manner, its stalked eyes swivelling as if worried that hundreds of neighbours are competing for the choicest morsels. At the alarm of a human or bird shadow falling their way, these crabs scuttle sideways comically en masse, each retreating to its own burrow in the mud.

There is safety in such numbers, but individually the little crabs are winkled out by certain fish, notably the snapper, snout burrowing in the silt on the flowing tide.

Ovalipes catharus, the common paddle or swimming crab of the inter-tidal zone.

135

As the tide ebbs several wading birds probe the mudflats with specially adapted beaks. The handsome oystercatcher, rather misnamed for it seldom 'catches' oysters, (more preferable is its onomatopoeic Maori name, torea, from its loud call) delves deep to extract hidden shellfish. It breaks open bivalves with hammer blows of its long, tough blunt-pointed scarlet bill. It is adept at locating the holes of burrowing species, and will drag forth marine worms, elastic creatures, in a tug of war which ends suddenly when the worm can no longer retain its tail grip on its mud tunnel.

More than a dozen migrant waders, which nest as far north as land exists in the northern Pacific-Arctic region, spend their winter - our summer - upon our estuarine flats. Day and night, according to lunar time, they alternate between feeding over low tide and roosting over the few hours of high water on favourite bare sand or shell banks with a wide view. Accustomed to nesting on the wide-open tundra, they are instinctively wary of predatory animals (wolf, fox, stoat, bear) capable of stalking them, and while with us they also sleep well away from cover.

Largest and most numerous of these visitors is the bar-tailed godwit, which plunges its long, slightly uptilted beak to

Bartailed godwits and salt-tolerant ice-plant *Disphyma australe*.

the hilt (close to the nostrils at the base) in watery mud, principally to obtain shell-less worms and other soft-bodied organisms. Its smaller, look-alike cousin, the knot, has the habit of flying and roosting in dense formation. With its shorter beak, the knot delves less deep for organisms near the surface. Many less common Arctic waders with interesting names, and bills of various shapes - short, stout, long, thin, upcurved, down-curved - adapted to specialised feeding, share this tidal habitat in peaceful coexisting groups: sandpipers, plovers, stilts, shanks, curlews, whimbrels, dotterels and tattlers.

The pied stilt, like the oystercatcher, is a resident wader, bold, noisy and beautiful with its contrasting pied plumage and bright pink legs trailing far behind in flight. It breeds plentifully on most wetlands throughout the country, but haunts the mudflats and coastal marshes in winter.

Black- and red-billed gulls with iceplant.

PRECEDING PAGES: Some visitors to the salt shore as seen by the artist: gannet, fur seal, dolphin and black-billed gull.

Tamest of all waders is the unique wrybill, hardly as large as a starling. It never leaves New Zealand, but flocks north in winter from its nesting grounds beside South Island rivers (*see page 97*). At Miranda in the Firth of Thames this pale grey and white wader is hard to see. At high tide it roosts idly on shellbanks and there you may almost step on it, as full-fed and sleepy it dozes on one leg. Its uniqueness lies in the tip of the dark bill being always twisted to the right. No one is quite sure why, but supposedly it may be an advantage in food searching under stones and debris, and as a kind of spoon when wading in shallow water after surface-swimming plankton.

Gulls of course are present on every shore, opportune scavengers of all flesh, live, disabled or dead, stranded along the tideline. They will gulp down your picnic scraps and a number may become sick and die through swallowing indigestible plastic food wrapping. Large flocks become parasitic at municipal waste dumps. However, although most numerous where they have easy access to such wastes, gulls are able to live independently, as they must have done in pre-Pakeha days, by fishing and beachcombing along the shore. In winter they may have to sustain fasts of a week or more in bad weather. Like vultures, they noisily concentrate when a teeming shoal of surface-swimming fish appears, perhaps mating or spawning, or in pursuit of a rising cloud of plankton composed of shrimp krill, newly-hatched whitebait or other small fish.

There are more than a dozen species or sub-species of cormorants or shags. Depicted here are three common species: the large black cormorant, the large pied and the little pied.

Dolphins are at the top of this assembly line of the ocean food chain, a magnificent sight as they breach and leap at the surface in unison, joyously pursuing kahawai, salmon, kingfish and other swift-swimming carnivores, which are in turn chasing the smaller mackerel, skipjack tuna, and snapper preying on the minute fish fry and shrimp (*Euphasid*) plankton.

Gannets are drawn to where the sea boils white as the shoals drive forward, pursued by birds above and dolphins and big fish below. On sighting a surface-swimming fish of the right size, the gannet checks in flight, staring downward with binocular vision and hovering briefly. Then with a few wing-flaps to gain momentum, it plunges vertically or at a steep angle, but streamlines its wings back in line with its tail - the line of least resistance to air and water. The gannet has inbuilt protection from the violent impact with the surface; it has no external nostrils up which water can be forced, its eyes are veiled with a clear (nictating) membrane, and a buffer of air cells cushions its lower neck feathers. The air cells also increase buoyancy under the water. The gannet must seize the fish swiftly, while the impetus of the dive lasts. In consequence, dives are short and shallow, and many are unsuccessful. Small fish are swallowed under water, thus avoiding piracy from hovering gulls and skuas; larger fish are brought, struggling, to the surface to be gulped down at risk of that piracy.

The Maori so prized the gannet as food that it had become scarce and confined to nesting on isolated off-shore rocks, difficult of access by the year 1769, when Captain Cook and botanist Joseph Banks first explored the New Zealand coast in the *Endeavour*. On Christmas Eve of that year Banks's diary records that he shot some gannets at sea close to the North Cape and 'on Christmas Day Goose pie was eat with great approbation and in the Evening all hands were as Drunk as our forefathers used to be on the like occasion.'

The gannet was also known to these men as the 'Solan goose', but they did not find any at Cape Kidnappers, where today, thanks to strict protection, there exists probably the largest mainland colony known. Under protection 110 years later, the first gannets settled there; today some 5000 pairs nest, out of a total of more than 46,000 pairs nesting along the whole of the New Zealand coast.

Male gannet with nesting material.

Juvenile gannet drawn from a dead specimen.

Sand Dunes

To see a world in a grain of sand,
And Heaven in a Wild Flower,
Hold Infinity in the palm of your hand,
And Eternity in an hour.
William Blake (1757-1827)

Sandy beaches are a scenic attraction of much of our long coast exposed to the prevailing gales of the Pacific Ocean and the Tasman Sea. In the absence of steep cliff barriers, such beaches are backed by extensive dunes of sand built up by wave action and blown inland. Here, tidal, solar and trade-wind rhythms, induced by the movements of the celestial bodies, including our planet, are made vivid. The immense area of horizon, the ceaseless murmur of the surf, the feeling of spacious solitude, impart a healing sense of freedom, nourishing the human spirit.

Here is the end and the beginning. The ocean thunders and booms upon the open beach, clouds are reflected in wet sand as each wave retreats; there is a momentary sea silence when you hear the faint clinking, crumbling of dry sand from the foredune edge; then the wild piping of a beach bird is drowned in the crash of the next surfing wave. In this symphony of sea and shore music you imagine you are listening to what the geologist tells us is actually taking place, but with infinite slowness; the rumbling of this tectonic (structurally changing) fragment of Gondwanaland plate which is New Zealand moving northwards - at a few millimetres a year - across the Pacific on its wandering flight towards the Equator from its ancient Antarctic origin, joined to Australia, untold millions of years ago.

On this lonely shore you are never lonely. Pausing to gaze from the height of a foredune on a calm day (avoid windy weather which whips dry grains of sand to sting your cheek) we admire the unending struggle between the steadfast land and the turbulent ocean. On such a day Earth edges nearer the sea. Long tentacles of newly-exposed roots of sand grasses - marram and the hardy native sedge, pingao *Desmoschoenus* - gravitate down bare slopes, seeking to re-root a sensitive living tip in some wind-free crevice, often under the accumulated jetsam of the high tide strand-line.

Sun and wind have dried the fine sand disturbed by our feet. It runs downhill as in an hour-glass. In this calm moment Earth seeks to return the hoarded dune-sand to rebuild gaps lately torn by storm-driven high tides. The tumbling grains expose and carry with them the minute fauna and seeds hidden below the

Local forms of copper butterflies are found throughout New Zealand, notably haunting low seaside vegetation.
The male in courtship displays both sides of his coppery-gold, black-spotted wings to the female, distinct by a lacy blue edging to her upper wings.

143

OPPOSITE: Lichens, pied oystercatcher, gulls in flight, seen from the sand-dunes.

OVER PAGE: More inhabitants of duneland country: redpoll finch and white-fronted terns. Native toe-toe grass enjoys the shelter of introduced lupin, an ideal sand-binder.

surface. If they reach the damp accumulation of the strand-line, where the little animals find cover, the seeds germinate in this favourable microclimate. Here the introduced pompom or tufted harestail grass, *Lagurs ovatus*, quickly establishes a mat of roots helping to bind the sand. A little higher up, in the spray zone but free of the highest waves, the curious silvery sand grass, *Spinifex hirsuta* is another sand stabiliser - curious because male and female grow as separate plants. The mature seed detaches in the form of the familiar spiked ball known as tumbleweed, carried hither and thither by every wind, tumbling and dancing until it meets an insurmountable obstacle - one of Nature's clever methods of ensuring wide dispersal of seed.

We have described the community of little, largely nocturnal salt-tolerant creatures inhabiting the strand-line of more sheltered coasts in 'The Tidal Shore', a habitat safe from the storms of the outer coast. Much the same vegetarian and carnivorous rubbish-eaters live in the tidal debris under the dunes, where the most abundant scavenger is the shrimp-like crustacean *Talorchestia quoyana*, a sandhopper which lurks by day in the shallow burrows it excavates under rotten seaweed.

Patiently nature builds, only to destroy. The next great gale on a high spring tide brings enormous, closely ranked waves to tear apart the greening carpet, to claw vertically at the foredune, each seething backwash dragging tonnes of sand down the beach. Depending on the direction of the wind and tidal flow, the displaced sand moves obliquely along the beach. On the west coast such storms are most frequent from the south and southwest, driving the sand-laden water northwards, eventually to reach the end of the land - at Farewell Spit in the South Island, and along the Ninety-Mile Beach to the North Cape in the North Island.

On east coast strands the Pacific swell under the prevailing land wind is gentler. It deposits sand to form bars across estuaries, and builds fewer dunes, except along the southeast coast exposed to chill Antarctic winds. It is estimated that dunes cover more than 120,000 hectares of coastal land and may spread several kilometres inland on low shores. Wind-dried sand from the unstable foredune, carried inland by persistent onshore gales, is swirled up and over quite steep slopes of older dunes, to be deposited in the lee, eddy or calm beyond the crest, maintaining and often increasing height.

Year by year such dunes move farther inland, and unless arrested by planting stabilising marram grass, lupins or pines, or all three in that sequence, relentlessly overwhelm lower ground with its often long-established bush and farmland. One such high moving dune is conspicuous near the northern entrance of Hokianga Harbour, dazzlingly white in fine weather, ochreous after rain. At present its further march is checked by the chafing effect of fast tides running over the bar in sight of dolphin-famous Opononi.

Dunes are of various colours: purest white where composed of pulverised shell (carbonate of lime); smoky dark on many west coast dunes, indicating the presence of iron oxide leached from the weathering of black beds of lava flows.

OPPOSITE: Pied stilts and white-faced herons stalk the shore and dune pools. The black oyster-catcher is a seashore species, resident and paired for life - slightly larger than its cousin the river-resting South Island pied oystercatcher.

Frustrated by steep cliffs above a shallow sea, wind-blown beach sand will accumulate and gradually build substantial foredunes in the cliff shadow. If the land mass here is uplifting under tectonic pressure, the new dune system advances seaward, becoming vegetated as the high-tide line recedes. A fine example of this is at Whatipu, under the cliffs of the Waitakere Ranges, west of Auckland. Here wind-gusts under the cliffs have removed sand to ground-water level, forming interesting small dune-enclosed lakes rich in wildlife - an enchanting place to wander and study on a fine summer day, with its backdrop of scarlet-flowering, pohutukawa-clad heights.

Heavy rain temporarily halts the movement of sand along the surface of the young unstable dune, but rapidly percolates and accumulates in the hollows long enough to encourage and nourish typical dune plants whose seeds are wind- or bird-carried. Pioneers are the yellow lupin, hairstail grass, sedges, muehlenbeckia, and red-berried *Tetragonia trigyna*, popularly known as New Zealand spinach. Where these hardy plants have begun to vegetate, the handsome native convolvulus, with parti-coloured pink and white flower trumpets, climbs profusely over the tops of their shoots during its intense midsummer flowering period, then its seed capsules wither away and the plant seems to disappear.

The half-clad dune, with its patches of wind-resistant vegetation, is the summer home of several shore birds. Conspicuous for its black livery and long scarlet bill and legs, is the black (also known as variable - some individuals are partly pied) oystercatcher, somewhat larger than its cousin, the South Island pied torea. It takes up a nesting territory here, convenient to its food supply of bivalves and other marine organisms obtained by delving at low tide in the sea's edge. The naked dune is scattered with thousands of empty shells, including those of cockles and pipis pried open by this oystercatcher. Little broken bits of shell often line the nest of the black torea, which is a mere scrape in the sand to accommodate the clutch of three eggs, neutrally marked in brown and buff to match the background. Both sexes incubate, but are extremely secretive on your approach. The sitting bird sneaks off at a warning pipe from the off-duty partner, but should you surprise the sitting bird amid the sand hummocks, it staggers away before you with trailing wings, apparently unable to fly. This is the 'broken wing trick' of many ground-nesting wading birds and ducks to lure a predator away from eggs or young. Once you have been enticed a sufficient distance, the enticer suddenly rises in flight, uttering a triumphant trill, maybe to inform its partner that the danger is past.

The same device is adopted by a much smaller and far less conspicuous wading bird, pale as the sand itself, the New Zealand dotterel, which is almost invisible when it crouches still. The two waders have interestingly different strategies for survival. The dotterel will not leave its four sand-coloured eggs until you have almost trodden on the incubating parent. As a strictly endemic bird evolved in a land free of predatory mammals, it developed its protective colour and habit of

The New Zealand dotterel

149

'freezing' when predatory birds were the only danger to its eggs or chicks, long before Man invaded the New Zealand paradise. Unfortunately, the dotterel has not yet learned that Man and his animal camp-followers have become its most lethal threat to survival. It continues to nest on sandy beaches and accessible dunes which are now popular recreation resorts of surfers, campers, sunbathers, and trail-bike clubs. Here we have seen picnickers lounging above the tide-line, unaware of a dotterel's bright eye watching them as it sits unmoving on its nest within a few metres. Here roaming children and keen-sighted and strong-nosed dogs also help to ensure that the dotterel will not rear any chicks. Yet some of the older dotterels persist; evidently this is 'home' to them. Marking this bird with leg-rings over the last forty years, ornithologists have proved that the dotterel can be long lived - some are still alive and breeding at over thirty years - in its main stronghold of Northland and the Hauraki Gulf beaches. There may be fewer than a thousand pairs breeding today here, and many fewer in the Foveaux Strait zone, 1200 kilometres southwards in a far colder climate.

The tern colony is synchronised in its social behaviour, almost to each day of the nesting period. Simultaneous arrival of the breeders, each quickly selecting a nuptial site, stimulates mating, egg-laying and hatching. This means that the larger the colony the greater the stimulus, the shorter the period of vulnerability to predation and the smaller in proportion the number of nests on its perimeter exposed to predators.

Caspian tern family

Like dotterel and torea, the sociable terns or sea swallows find safer nesting sanctuary in remote, little-visited sand dunes. There is abundant summer food obtained by shallow plunges or snatches upon the surface-swimming shoals of sprats and small immature fish close inshore. In courtship, the male tern brings a fish to the nest site, holding it in the bill for several minutes as a token of love and his invitation to mate.

The large Caspian tern, stocky and gull-like, has a cosmopolitan range, but is not a migrant in New Zealand. After nesting in small groups, it leaves the dunes to spend the rest of the year fishing near, and roosting within, large estuaries and mudflats. The young Caspians accompany their parents for several weeks, mewing for food. You recognise the adult by its harsh yakkity-yak call in flight, its large crimson bill, and, in summer, its jet black monk's cap pulled down to the eye and bill. In winter this cap is a mottled grey-white, like that of the juvenile.

Smaller, daintier and sveltely beautiful, New Zealand's endemic sea swallow *Sterna striata*, known as the white-fronted

tern, its lower forehead being white, has a long forked tail, black feet and bill, and the monk's cap tilted back to cover the nape. It is numerous from North Cape to the sub-Antarctic islands. It nests in dunes, on rocky islets, cliffs, even on breakwaters, so long as these sites are reasonably safe from human and other predators. On dunes, where up to a hundred pairs may assemble to breed, they are more vulnerable to ground predators, but if these attack too freely, the whole colony may move to a new site, if necessary abandoning the surviving eggs and young nestlings.

Terns seem capricious in this respect. They betray their presence at colonies by a continuous noisy calling on sighting your approach, and stay hovering overhead. Gradually most of them settle back to their nests when you sit quietly at the edge of the colony. Even so and for no visible reason, you will find the whole flock suddenly, simultaneously, rising at intervals in complete silence for perhaps four seconds, before again uttering their harsh, excited calls as they return to domestic duties. This simultaneous manoeuvre has been called a 'panic' or 'dread' by tern watchers, suggesting a momentary reassertion of the flocking instinct.

Do not walk about within the tern colony, for not only is this unfair, by causing unnecessary disturbance, but you may be viciously attacked. A hundred adult terns simultaneously stabbing you with their sharp, pointed bills might inflict bloody wounds on your unprotected head, but in fact communally nesting seabirds never attack simultaneously. Each pair attacks the intruder only when the territory around its nest is invaded. In this way they can scare off fox, dog, cat, gull, and usually the unwary human trespasser not wearing a crash helmet. A tourist in chill Spitzbergen one day came back to the ship with his bald head spouting blood from direct hits from the dagger bills of a pair of Arctic terns, which are similar in size to our white-fronted species.

Farther inland, beyond the bared pale sand with its tufts of invading vegetation, the dune becomes stabilised with an increasingly shrubby growth of wind-resistant plants gradually dominating the grasses and sedges: lupins, prickly tangles of *Muehlenbeckia complexa, Coprosma acerosa* (which has transparent, pale blue berries), sand daphne *Pimilia arenaria*, and here and there alien gorse, self-sown radiata pine, and Australian wattle. It is a knee- or waist-high dune forest as yet, with the chestnut-coloured shafts and nodding heads of native toe-toe grass lifting clear.

Seed-eating redpolls have colonised this windy shrubbery; these small inconspicuous fast-flying, restless finches are hard to get a close-up view of with binoculars. They nest here as freely as they do in the bushline of alpine country. The male has a rosy throat in summer, and both sexes wear a black bib and red poll or pate. Look for the neat cup of the nest woven into the top of a shrub. Two or more broods are reared each summer.

Although few but ornithologists know this mercurial bird, it is increasing rapidly where it can feed upon a mixture of the seeds of alien and native plants, and in winter will appear in suburbs to feast on the winged seed of silver birch.

OPPOSITE: White-fronted terns in flight. Gannet skull and scarab beetle in foreground.

OVER PAGE: Redpolls at nest.

153

The sea wind can be cool and strong as it blows over the surface of the low dune scrub, but usually there are gaps and paths where you can enjoy lying flat on the sandy ground in a sheltered, warm microclimate, studying the interesting inhabitants of this stratum: sometimes deer, always hedgehogs, lizards, and moths.

Two small, inconspicuous brown birds are ground feeders here, sharing the lowly habitat without much competition for the food supply - numerous insects and molluscs. Snails of many species, large and small, flourish in this cover above the lime-rich sand which contributes calcium for shell-making through the snails' plant diet. Both birds eat seeds and small berries in season, and both have thin, whispering songs. One is the New Zealand pipit, described earlier (*see page 106*). The other, the dunnock - misnamed hedge-sparrow - sings throughout the year, save during the late summer moult. Introduced from Britain in the last century, the dunnock has spread throughout New Zealand, even to the sub-Antarctic Campbell Islands - surprisingly, since it appears reluctant to fly. It feeds on the ground, searching this closely as it moves with a shuffling movement of its feet, and frequently flicking its wings - hence its alternative name, shufflewing.

Although found sparsely in suburban shrubberies and large gardens, it is more numerous in low scrub-covered ground near the sea. We have a special affection for this confiding mousey-looking bird as a companion when we have lived on remote islands. Despite its unobtrusive habits, it is strongly territorial. The constant wheedling song of the cock is a challenge to rival males to keep away from his home pitch, and a reminder to his hen of his whereabouts therein. In courtship, both shuffle and flick their wings in an excited display. Mating occurs during a mutual ceremony of tail-lifting and inspection of the genital areas. A cock sings as a rule from the top of low vegetation, in which the hen builds a neat cup nest for her four to five eggs, which are a beautiful clear sea-blue.

OPPOSITE: Dunnock collecting nest material in a wild peach tree. The hen incubates the eggs alone, but her mate helps to feed the chicks.

BELOW: Native convolvulus

The Endless Little Isles

O these endless little isles
lying clad in soft verdure,
and in thine awful solitude,
afar off in the lap of wild ocean,
not to see thee with the carnal eye,
will be to have seen nothing!
                    T.S. Muir (1836 - 1914)

So may the fortunate feel who have visited some of the endless little islands over which New Zealand claims sovereignty: at least 600 of them, stretching between the near-tropical Kermadecs in the lap of wild ocean to the north at 29/31ºS, and cool, windy Campbell Island, 3600 kilometres distant at 52º 33' S in the sub-Antarctic ocean. Many of these fit Shakespeare's description from *The Tempest:* 'The isle is full of noises, sounds, and sweet airs, that give delight, and hurt not.' From time immemorial our oceanic islands have been full of noises, day and night, uttered by vast numbers of nesting seabirds which exploit the rich marine food chain of upwelling seas around New Zealand, where the subtropical currents of northern origin converge and clash with cold currents from the south. Isolated in this rich zone 1600 kilometres from the land mass of Australia, our numerous small islands provide the only convenient nesting refuge for many ocean-going seabirds, especially albatrosses, shearwaters, and the several species of large and small gadfly, prion and storm petrels. This extensive family, known as the Tubinares from their prominent tubular nostrils above the strong hooked beak, never voluntarily alight on the land, save at nesting time. They never drink fresh water. To dispose of surplus salt taken with their fish prey, the nostrils are specially adapted to excrete this through glands at the base of the bill so that beads of salt solution run down the external grooves to drip from the point of the down-curved bill.

We recall summer nights lying among the tangled native shrubs near the summit (722m) of mountainous, ravined Hauturu (Little Barrier Island) in the Hauraki Gulf, listening with delight to the excited, twittering calls of the titi (as the Maori call the dove-sized Cook's petrel) flying home from its far-wandering feeding voyage. As the sun sank behind the low horizon of Northland, 24 kilometres distant across the dolphin-haunted sea, a heavy dew descended from a cloudless sky. The wind-resistant flowers of this rocky summit - snowberry and the rare *Metrosideros parkinsonii* (a small, scarlet-flowered pohutu-kawa named after New Zealand's first artist, on Cook's

Blue penguin

OPPOSITE: Three New Zealand penguins: (top) Fiordland *Eudyptes pachyrhynchus*; yellow-eyed *Megadyptes antipodes* (centre and left); and white-flippered *Eudyptula albosignata* (bottom right).

159

Pycroft's petrel and the fluttering shearwater

Endeavour) - were closed for the night. The shrill 'kiwi' call of a male bird echoed from a ravine far below.

Earlier that evening we had heard cries of seabirds flocking offshore as they awaited nightfall. Now, almost suddenly, there was a roar of titi calls as the first flock of Cook's petrels swept overhead, swirling close around the summit rocks, then thumping noises as individual petrels landed, some crashing through the vegetation. With hardly a pause each bird vanished into burrows and rock-holes. The first to return are always mated birds anxious to get home - to egg or sitting partner, or to feed and brood a chick. For this small gadfly petrel there is also the risk of being snapped up by a predator above ground. Later in the night, and season, the unemployed pre-breeder petrels, without a partner, young and inexperienced, will land, and for a while sit about in the open. This is a period, perhaps lasting several seasons, of familiarising themselves with a future breeding site and mate.

The calls of more flocks circling home lasted a full half hour. Many thousands must have landed on Hauturu. Among them a few of the much larger black petrel alighted silently and ran past us, light-footed, goblin-like in this ghostly approach, and vanished swiftly into the rocky ground. A muffled clacking conversation with mate or nestling ensued.

As long ago as 1894 Little Barrier was declared a nature reserve, purchased from its Maori owners, but these left behind goats and gone-wild cats, the latter a serious control problem on this large (2817 hectares) island heavily timbered and full of steep ravines. It was the last home in the world of the beautiful stitchbird, a honey-eater with a brush-tipped tongue like the bellbird, its close but slightly larger relative. Feral cats had reduced these to dangerously low numbers, despite energetic hunting by the resident ranger with gun and dog. On our first visit in 1974 the higher ground was littered with the cat-killed remains of Cook's petrels. We helped the campaign to live-trap the cats along the few tracks established at that time, but it was not until nine years later that, with the knowledge that the cats find it convenient to walk, stalk and conduct their love affairs on such tracks, teams of workers were enlisted to open up a system of tracks around the whole island. After these had been

Once upon a time most of the islands of New Zealand were inhabited by one of the world's oldest reptiles, the tuatara, a miniature crested dragon in appearance, an archaic, slow-moving creature not altered much since the 'Time of the Terrible Dragons', that is the dinosaurs, which became extinct many millions of years ago. Its bones have been recovered from early Maori middens, limestone caves and buried in sand dunes, from Cape Reinga to the Bluff, but it was unable to coexist with Man and his animal followers. Only on small islands free of these today does the tuatara survive: some twenty islets in the Hauraki Gulf, the Bay of Plenty, and Cook Strait. Here you may be fortunate to see, as we have, the tuatara basking close to the entrance to its burrow, where it usually rests by day. At night it actively searches for insects, wetas, moths and other small life. It often shares a burrow with a small shearwater or petrel commonly nesting on such islands free of ground predators. Strange bedfellows found sitting together underground amicably, although occasionally the little dragon has been known to swallow a newly-hatched petrel chick. The female tuatara lays up to a dozen eggs in the spring, covers them with earth, then forgets them. The embryos develop during the ensuing summer, but virtually hibernate over the chill winter months. This long diapause results in an 'in-shell' period of a whole year. Like the tortoise, this cool-blooded, lethargic reptile is reputed to live much longer than a human.

The South Island saddleback

laboriously cut up and down the steep ravines, the last cat was eliminated.

There has been a splendid recovery of all the native birds since - so much so that stitchbirds are plentiful enough for a nucleus of breeding stock to be translocated to other cat-free islands in the Hauraki Gulf. Also, the flightless night-parrot or kakapo, on the point of extinction elsewhere, the blue-wattled, weak-winged kokako, now rare in mainland native forests, and the lively but also weak-winged saddleback, have been established on Little Barrier as an insurance against extinction. All three have settled down well, and begun to breed.

This success story has not been possible on the neighbouring, very much larger island of Great Barrier, long farmed and settled by Maori and Pakeha colonists. Its once abundant native wildlife is much depleted by the black or ship rat, which came ashore from cargo and whaling ships more than a century ago. *Rattus rattus* is a nimble tree-climber, an opportunist feeding alike on leaves, fruit, insects, and the eggs and chicks of birds. As a result the tree-nesting kokako is nearly extinct, but the powerfully-beaked kaka or bush parrot seems to hold its own, defending its nest in a tree-hole.

162

One of the main attractions of Great Barrier are its swamps and little rivers. Here the scarce brown duck survives in small flocks, free at least of mustelids - although there are wild pigs and feral cats. This sober-looking duck is nocturnal, but very tame, sleeping by day where you may study it along the banks of streams, and much loved and strictly protected by the Islanders. The large swamps harbour good numbers of bittern and fernbirds.

Scenically Great Barrier is very beautiful with high hills, little farms and remnant kauri forest. We have camped on its highest peak (621m) on a summer night, seeking the petrels which formerly bred in great numbers here, but found only a few pairs of Cook's and the black species surviving in nigh-inaccessible crannies.

Rugged, mountainous Kapiti Island guards the northern approach to Cook Strait. Early in the last century it became the fortified retreat of the notorious warrior, Te Rauparaha, who encouraged and profited by visiting whale hunters. In a few decades the giant whales migrating through Cook Strait were virtually exterminated. As at Great Barrier Island these ships brought rats - this time the larger brown *Rattus norvegicus*, which does not climb trees - so Kapiti's tree-nesting birds were unaffected.

Among domestic and other animals introduced were cattle, goats, sheep, cats, opossums, and wekas. Also, but almost by chance, a few little spotted kiwis were released. When Kapiti was declared a public nature reserve in 1897 this kiwi, now extinct on the mainland, was present on the island in sufficient strength, despite the rats (and opossums which like to lie up by day in kiwi burrows), to rebuild the present strong population on Kapiti. Domestic animals were removed, allowing the native forest, bruised by browsing, to recover. Native trees and plants have been encouraged, and opossums and cats controlled to low numbers; possibly they may eventually be eliminated. It is now hoped to transfer surplus little spotted kiwi to other island reserves, such as Tiri-tiri in the Hauraki Gulf. One of the first 'open' island wildlife sanctuaries to anyone who will respect the regulations for landing, Tiri-tiri needs to be secure from rats, cats and other alien introductions. Saddlebacks and native parakeets are already flourishing there from recent releases. Saddlebacks have also been restored to Kapiti, but may be in trouble from the introduced weka. Although the flightless weka will kill and eat young rats, it also preys on any small bird it can surprise on the ground, and the saddleback is largely a ground-feeder.

Kapiti is a good island to visit. We have spent happy hours studying its flourishing community of birds, typically tame from long protection. Around the ranger's cottage kaka parrots will land on your hand or head if you offer a raisin. Robin, tomtit, fantail and silver-eye flutter around you, snatching up insects disturbed by your stroll along forest tracks; above, the parakeets chatter as they fly from fruiting treetops, and native pigeons clatter and wing-loop noisily. Long-tailed cuckoos screech from high trees; these long-distance migrants come from northern tropical islands, seeking to mate, and presently the hens will lay

The scarce brown duck *Anas chlorotis* is nocturnal and unique to New Zealand.

Little blue or fairy penguin

their eggs in the nests of whitehead warblers, plentifully resident on Kapiti, as are tui, bellbird, kingfisher, rifleman and morepork, as well as most of the European birds. Along the low eastern shore black oystercatchers maintain territories. The island also has colonies of red-billed gulls and white-fronted terns, and blue penguins occupy burrows under flax or holes in the bouldery slopes.

Sleeping one night on the small islets close inshore here, we listened to loud-cooing sooty shearwaters and the sweeter twittering of the white-faced storm petrel. The latter is known of old to sailors as the 'J.C. Bird', a term derived from the same source as 'petrel' - St Peter's bird. St Peter walked on water, or was invited by Jesus Christ to do so. This little storm petrel collects food as it patters over the sea with webbed feet lightly touching the waves.

If you are able to climb across Kapiti Island to the sheer western cliffs by nightfall, there is the same bedlam of tubenose calls as at Little Barrier, chiefly from in-flight muttonbirds which nest in the inaccessible rock walls; sooty and fluttering shear-waters and perhaps smaller petrels.

On our cruise in 1981 between Antarctica and Stewart Island we were lucky to have fine summer weather for landing upon New Zealand's southernmost island. Campbell, 1133 hectares, was first discovered in 1810 by sealers, who wiped out the huge herds of fur and elephant seals in these areas. Next to be massacred was *Balaena glacialis*, the massive black right whale, so-called because it was the 'right' whale to hunt; slow-moving, covered with a thick blubber rich in oil, it did not sink when killed. Fortunately this species was not entirely wiped out. It entered the deep fiords which penetrate Campbell Island to give birth to its tonne-weight calf in midwinter, when storms kept the whale hunters away. Now a nucleus has returned, is slowly increasing, and some of the well-grown, non-breeding adolescents of this majestic black sea-giant are spending their juvenile years northwards, off the mainland New Zealand coast. So splendidly tame is this whale that you may approach and touch one in a small boat as it browses close inshore on krill and little fishes. We have a photograph of one which liked to accompany a Kaikoura fishing smack, and permitted the crew to ride on its back! It has little to fear from Man in the new 200-mile offshore zone under New Zealand's control, save occasional entanglement in seining and other large nets - an accident not always reported by the net-owner if the whale is drowned. It is strictly protected world-wide.

The cold, wet climate and remote situation defeated attempts between 1895 and 1931 to farm Campbell Island with cattle and sheep. It was declared a nature reserve in 1954. Today numerous shags, thousands of rockhopper and yellow-eyed penguins, gulls and albatrosses breed there.

Campbell Island is still overrun with brown rats escaped from the verminous whaling ships. These have eliminated all small burrowing shearwaters and petrels, save on the inaccessible cliffs. However, larger animals and birds are unaffected by this.

PRECEDING PAGES: Most of the small islands off the coasts of New Zealand provide nesting cover in the low cliffs and wind-blown vegetation for little blue penguins, red-billed gulls and shags.

On Campbell Island there is a small meteorological station in the shelter of Perseverance Inlet - the calm waters of the whale nursery. Five men have made a home-from-home of the little wooden structure, planting around it hardy native flax, spiderwood *Dracophyllum* and majestic clumps of the Antarctic daisy, *Pleurophyllum*, with huge rosetted leaves and brown-centred pink flowers. Only a few cattle and sheep are left today, pastured on the fenced-off western peninsula. This is to the advantage of the world's largest albatrosses - *Diomedea exulans*, the wanderer, and *D. epomophora*, the royal. With very long narrow wings spanning over 3.5 metres, they prefer smooth ground for taking off, which in calm weather requires a long taxiing run clear of obstacles. The ungrazed two-thirds of this island is a chest-high tangle of hardy shrubs, in which we blundered upon fur and elephant and Hooker's seals in their smelly, moulting wallows.

'As big as turkeys!' gasped my cruise companion, Richard Adams, as we climbed the smooth, grazed sward under Mt Honey (567 m). He was unprepared for the magnificent sight of hundreds of noble albatrosses sitting tranquilly on their pedestal nests, brooding the single egg or chick. 'Their beauty is like that of cliffs and caves,' he wrote in his diary. 'Their sheer size is startling as they sit on their tall castles of earth and wispy grass. Their demeanour towards us showed no hostility or alarm, but on the contrary gave the impression of magnanimously sparing us a little attention provided we behaved perfectly ...'

So tame are these giants at the nest, as we have studied them at Campbell, Auckland, Macquarie and South Georgia Islands, that we have been able to stroke them, after an interval of sitting quietly near and gaining their confidence. We were shown how to do this on our first visit to the royal albatross colony on Taiaroa Head, near Dunedin, more than twenty years ago. The ranger, Stan Sharpe, continuing the banding study initiated by pioneering Lawrence Richdale in the 1930s, freely stroked one old favourite he called Grandma, gently lifting her breast to see if the white egg - identity number scribbled thereon - had hatched. Grandma, by the way, is reported to be still alive and breeding, as we write this. She must be all of sixty years old, allowing her around ten years for her adolescent non-breeding years.

Taiaroa is claimed to be the only known colony of these huge albatrosses on any mainland coast in the world. It is now protected by a strong fence from interference, but from a comfortable warm hut you may watch the group of nesting royals on this grassy headland. Information today (1987) is that Grandma, now alleged to be the oldest known banded bird on record, has, in shared duty with her present mate, a younger bird, hatched this year's chick. Ten other pairs are nesting; and eighteen unemployed albatrosses are frequent visitors - which means that the colony is some twenty mature breeders strong. As these albatrosses take a full year to rear one replacement (one month courtship and nest-building, average of seventy-five days incubation, and another 257 days while the chick remains in the nest), they are only able to breed successfully once in two years.

Royal albatross

Banding has shown they need a sabbatical year to recover, during which royal and wandering albatrosses glide almost effortlessly, rarely flapping their wings, on the lift of the strong trade winds of the Roaring Forties, thousands of kilometres east around the world in those latitudes. So do the newly-fledged young. After enduring their long first winter on the pedestal nest through snow and gales, they sail away to spend several years fancy-free and wandering, sleeping at sea, but never on land. In due course, the maturing bird, seeking to mate, circles back to the well-remembered birthplace to find one - in a ceremonial greeting dance which breaks down the loneliness of the years of adolescent seafaring.

Unfrequented shores difficult of human access remain sanctuaries for nesting seabirds. The common silver gull of our coast, the red-billed *Larus scopulinus*, builds its substantial nest handy to the sea on isolated stacks and often amid the tangle of the highest strand-line. Here it may be partly sheltered by background vegetation such as the orange-berried *Coprosma repens,* or on Northland shores, by the splendid crimson blossom of ancient pohutukawa trees with one foot in the water. On treeless islands in the far south, the nest may be tucked into the mouth of a cave. The two brown-scribbled eggs are incubated by both sexes; probably the pair mates for life once it has established a nest site.

On that cruise from Antarctica we next visited the less chill, partly forested Auckland Isles, refuge of a flightless form of the brown duck. This lives largely on marine organisms in the tidal zone dominated by the immense long tresses of *Durvillea* kelp. The northern island of Enderby was once farmed by an English whaling company which set up a small base - Port Ross - on the main island just opposite. This was abandoned in 1852 on the failure of the whaling. We found Enderby ringing with the songs of bellbirds and tuis in flowering rata bush, under which nesting albatrosses and Hooker's sea lions and their pups make interesting bedfellows, with tomtits, moulting penguins and the absurdly tame pipits, native snipe and parakeets. Fortunately there are no rats. Rabbits, introduced by Sir James Ross on his polar visit in 1840, are an astonishing blue colour - possibly the result of inbreeding. The fierce New Zealand falcon and the Antarctic skua seem to keep their numbers under control.

And so to the lonely, rarely visited Snares Islands, 210 kilometres south of Bluff, remarkable for three unique land birds: an all-black tomtit (opposite), a sub-Antarctic snipe, and a

large subspecies of fernbird. The last is oddly adapted to catching flies attracted to the bodies of seals resting and moulting under the wind-battered olearia and senecio scrub. There are no cats or rats. This small 243 hectare group is crammed with thousands of burrow-nesting petrels, with huge colonies of the Snares crested penguin and the Snares mollymawk (small albatross), *Diomedea bulleri*. Rock-bound and difficult of access in stormy seas, it is a closed nature reserve, one of the finest in the world.

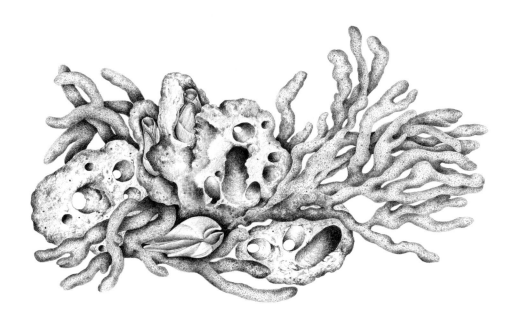

INDEX